Max Planck

Uncovering the World of Matter

Jane Weir, MPhys

Physical Science Readers:

Max Planck: Uncovering the World of Matter

Publishing Credits

Editorial Director
Dona Herweck Rice

Associate Editor
Joshua BishopRoby

Editor-in-Chief
Sharon Coan, M.S.Ed.

Creative Director
Lee Aucoin

Illustration Manager
Timothy J. Bradley

Publisher
Rachelle Cracchiolo, M.S.Ed.

Science Contributor
Sally Ride Science

Science Consultants
Michael E. Kopecky,
Science Department Chair,
Chino Hills High School
Jane Weir, MPhys

Teacher Created Materials
5301 Oceanus Drive
Huntington Beach, CA 92649-1030
http://www.tcmpub.com

ISBN 978-0-7439-0568-8

Table of Contents

The End of Science?

Max Karl Ernst Ludwig Planck (plahnk) was born on April 23, 1858, in Germany. At that time, people thought they had solved all the big problems in science. Planck's teachers told him that there was no point in studying science. They thought there wasn't anything much left to learn! They said he should study math.

Planck didn't listen to them. He went to a university to study **physics**. Physics is the science that studies **matter** and **energy**. It explores what everything is made of, how it moves, and how it changes.

Planck as a young man

It's a good thing he didn't listen. The twentieth century turned out to be very busy for scientists. And a lot of new things were learned because of Planck!

In 1918, Max Planck won the Nobel Prize for his discovery of quanta (page 18). He became world famous and known as the Father of Quantum Physics.

Planck's studies opened new worlds in science for others to study.

Growing Up

Max Planck was the sixth child born to Johann and Emma Planck. They gave him every opportunity to study and learn. And Planck loved to learn.

Planck came from a family of very smart, hardworking people. Some of them were professors, lawyers, and judges. They taught him to think for himself. They taught him to work hard. That's just what Planck spent his life doing.

Planck read a great deal to learn from the work of other scientists.

Munich around the time Planck lived there with his family

Learning was a bright light in Planck's life. When he was nine years old, his family moved to Munich (MYOO-nik), Germany. One teacher took Planck under his wing. He taught the boy math as well as mechanics and astronomy. Planck first learned about energy from this teacher. Planck studied so hard that he graduated early from school. He was just 16 years old.

But there was a cloud over Planck's childhood. One of his earliest memories was of war. Troops marched through his hometown during the German-Danish war. War was a part of Planck's childhood. It would become a tragic part of his adulthood, too.

Music or Science?

Planck studied music, too. He was a talented singer. He also played the piano, organ, and cello. He wrote songs and operas. He thought about having a career in music. But science won out. He gave up his study of music to focus on science instead.

New Ideas

Planck studied at the University of Munich. A physics teache there told him not to study physics! The teacher said, "In this field almost everything is already discovered .... All that remains is to f a few holes." Planck didn't want to discover new things. He wante to learn about what was known. So, he studied and led experimen about what others had figured out.

The more he learned, the more he thought about things. He went to Berlin to study with the famous scientists there. He began to study **theories** of physics. Theories are explanations. They are ways of thinking about and analyzing something to understand what you cannot see.

Physics Hall at the University of Munich

Planck found he didn't want to do experiments anymore. He wanted to explain why things are as they are. He took what was known and used it to help understand what wasn't known. H proved there was a whole lot left to lear in science.

Planck studied matter and its properties. This led him to learn what happens to matter in different conditions. Matter and heat really interested him. All of Planck's studies led him to choose heat theory as his fie He would go on to make big discoverie about matter and heat.

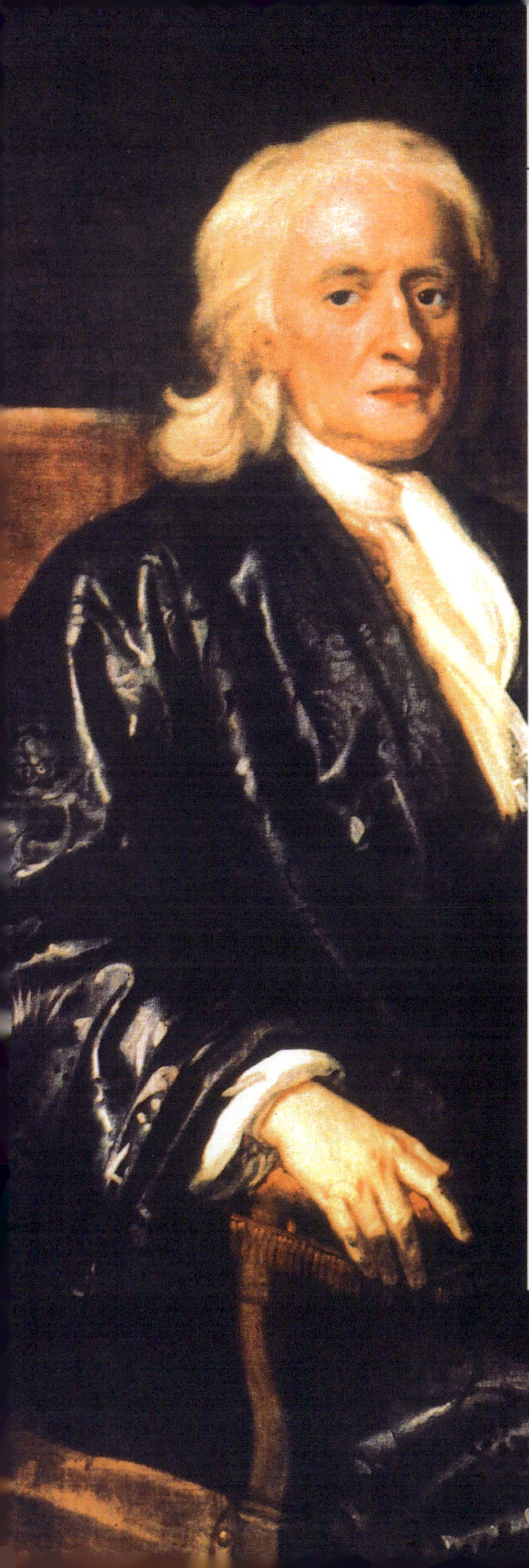

From Newton to New Ideas

Sir Isaac Newton (1642-1727) was born and raised in England. He was a great scientist and mathematician. He was also a scholar of history. Many people think of him as the founder of modern physical science. He spent his life dedicated to his work.

Newton's work was the basis of study for many scientists who came after him. He was among the most important scientists studied by Max Planck. Many scientists of Planck's time thought Newton had figured everything out. They believed Newton had discovered nearly everything there was left to discover. They were wrong. Planck and other great scientists of modern times have proven that there is always more to learn when it comes to science.

Heat and Movement

The study of heat and how it moves is called **thermodynamics** (thur-moh-dye-NAM-iks). This became Planck's main field of study. He knew that heat doesn't just stay in one place. It moves. It gets passed from one thing to another. This may sound very simple, but there are some big ideas behind this simple concept. It became Planck's job to figure them out.

Matter is the "stuff" that makes up the contents of the universe. Matter is made of tiny particles called **atoms**. No one can see an atom. That takes a very powerful microscope. But atoms are the basis of matter, no matter what. How the atoms join together is what makes something unique. How the atoms move has a lot to do with heat.

Heat is all around us and in us. It is in the sun and radiating from it. It is in our bodies, too.

Jane Goodall

Animal Scientist and Friend

Connie Jankowski

Life Science Readers:
Jane Goodall: Animal Scientist and Friend

Publishing Credits

Editorial Director
Dona Herweck Rice

Creative Director
Lee Aucoin

Associate Editor
Joshua BishopRoby

Illustration Manager
Timothy J. Bradley

Editor-in-Chief
Sharon Coan, M.S.Ed.

Publisher
Rachelle Cracchiolo, M.S.Ed.

Science Contributor
Sally Ride Science™

Science Consultants
Thomas R. Ciccone, B.S., M.A.Ed.,
Chino Hills High School
Dr. Ronald Edwards,
DePaul University

Teacher Created Materials
5301 Oceanus Drive
Huntington Beach, CA 92649-1030
http://www.tcmpub.com
ISBN 978-0-7439-0594-7

Table of Contents

Goodall's Never-Ending Journey

Jane Goodall is an authority on chimpanzees. In fact, she is the world's leading authority. She once lived in a comfortable home. Then, she left it all to live in the jungle. She gave up modern conveniences. She lived in conditions that few would tolerate. She followed her heart. She found peace and friendship living in Africa. She found a world filled with fascinating creatures.

Goodall has devoted her life to learning about chimps. Her work has been in journals and books. She has even been on television shows. Her work is respected worldwide. She has become a model for others to follow.

Fun Fact

Goodall's father bought her a special gift for her second birthday. He gave her a toy chimp. It was lifelike. She named it Jubilee. She named it after a baby chimp at the London Zoo. To this day, it is one of Goodall's prized possessions.

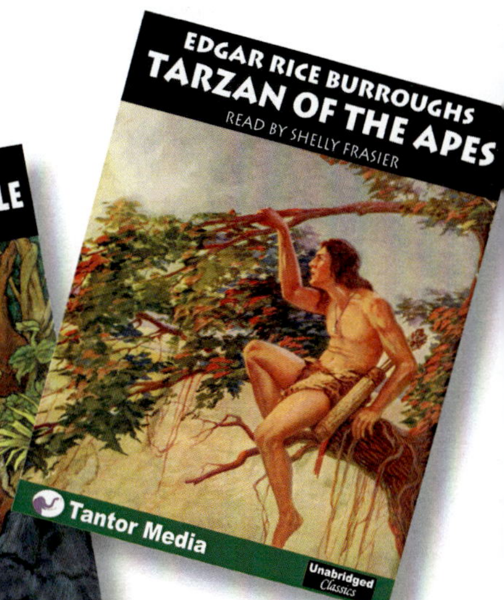

Fun Fact

Jane Goodall's favorite childhood books were *Dr. Doolittle* and *Tarzan*.

Goodall on Chimps

"The long hours spent with them in the forest have enriched my life beyond measure. What I have learned from them has shaped my understanding of human **behavior**, of our place in nature."

The Early Years

Goodall was born in 1934. She lived in England. When she was five, World War II broke out in Europe. Her father went off to war. Her parents divorced shortly afterward.

Her mother moved the family to the country. They lived with Goodall's grandmother. Gooddall was fascinated with the animals she found in the country. She played with her grandmother's pets. She explored the wildlife around her. She loved riding horses.

Goodall tried many jobs before she found her true calling. When she was 23, she left England on a boat to Africa. One of her friends had family in Kenya. She was going to have a great trip. Her visit lasted almost two

Goodall with her younger sister

Did You Know?

As a child, Goodall and her friends liked animal adventures. They formed a club when she was 12. It was called the Alligator Society. They did different activities. They did nature projects, games and quizzes. They even made *The Alligator Society Magazine* to entertain themselves!

years. She took jobs to support herself. She explored the countryside. Then, a friend took Goodall to visit a famous **paleontologist**. His name was Louis Leaky. The visit changed Goodall's life.

A Mother's Advice

Goodall credits success to her mother. Her mother was a well-known author. Her name was Vanne Goodall. She must have seen stars in young Goodall's eyes. She knew how much her daughter loved animals and adventures. Girls were expected to follow certain paths. Many mothers would have squashed their daughters' dreams. But Mrs. Goodall told her child to live her dreams. She told her to never give up.

These paleontologists are uncovering the remains of a mammoth.

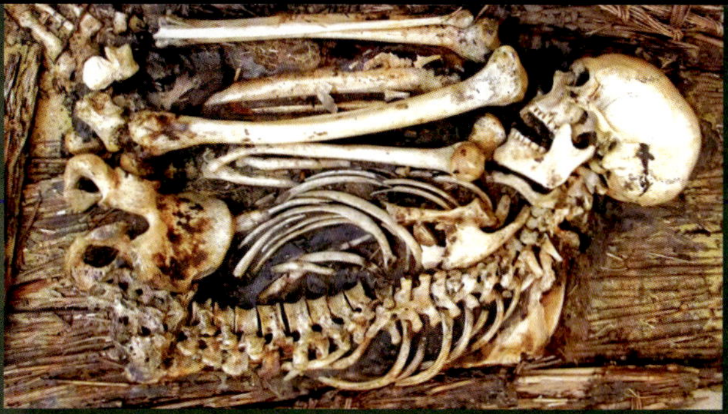

Ethology

Ethology is the study of animal behavior.

Mentor

Leakey **mentored** Goodall. He helped her establish goals. He prepared her for a rugged life. At times he provided moral support. He helped raise money to fund her studies. He introduced her to people who could help. He became a father figure to Goodall. Their "family" held together for more than 30 years.

Leakey wanted to study apes. He thought it would be useful in understanding early humans. Goodall told Leakey about her love for animals. Leakey thought she would be perfect for the research. She wasn't a trained scientist. She didn't have any preformed ideas. He thought she would be free to observe the truth. So he gave her a job.

Leakey and Goodall's family helped her set up camp. They started in 1960. Leakey knew the work would not be easy. It would take a special person to make such a huge commitment. The study would take many years. Time was needed to set up camp. She needed to earn the trust of the apes. More time was needed to see them grow and develop relationships. She needed to observe their **social** interactions.

Goodall studied the chimps for more than 30 years. She learned all she could about their world.

Leakey studied early humans by observing and testing their remains and artifacts.

Louis Leaky (1903–1972)

Leakey was one of the world's greatest explorers. He learned about early humans. He found many fossils and stone tools in Africa. His work convinced others that the first humans walked in Africa.

Leakey encouraged Jane to study the chimps' behavior. He wanted to learn about their habits and their relationships. He wanted to know about their ability to think and solve problems. He wanted to know about their families. He wanted to know about friendships and enemies. He wanted details to compare to human behavior.

Leakey helped start the careers of some great **primatologists**. He coached Jane Goodall in her work. He also **mentored** Dian Fossey. She worked with mountain gorillas. He established Biruté Galdikas as a field scientist. She works with orangutans.

Field Research

Goodall waited patiently until the chimpanzees let her get close. Sometimes the chimps got really close, too!

Goodall arrived in Tanzania in the summer of 1960. She was ready to study the chimpanzees. They did not greet her warmly. The chimps ran whenever they saw her. She never gave up. She kept her distance. She watched through binoculars.

Goodall tried to fit in with the group. She kept as quiet as possible. She learned to do things like the chimps. She knew to wait for the chimps to show they were ready. She didn't want to push herself on them. Her patience paid off. The chimps slowly accepted her. Little by little, the chimpanzees became comfortable with her. They came closer and closer.

After a few months, she watched two chimps strip leaves from a branch. They used the branch as a tool. They used it to pull termites out of a nest. This showed that chimps are more intelligent than was thought before. Scientists thought using tools was something only humans could do.

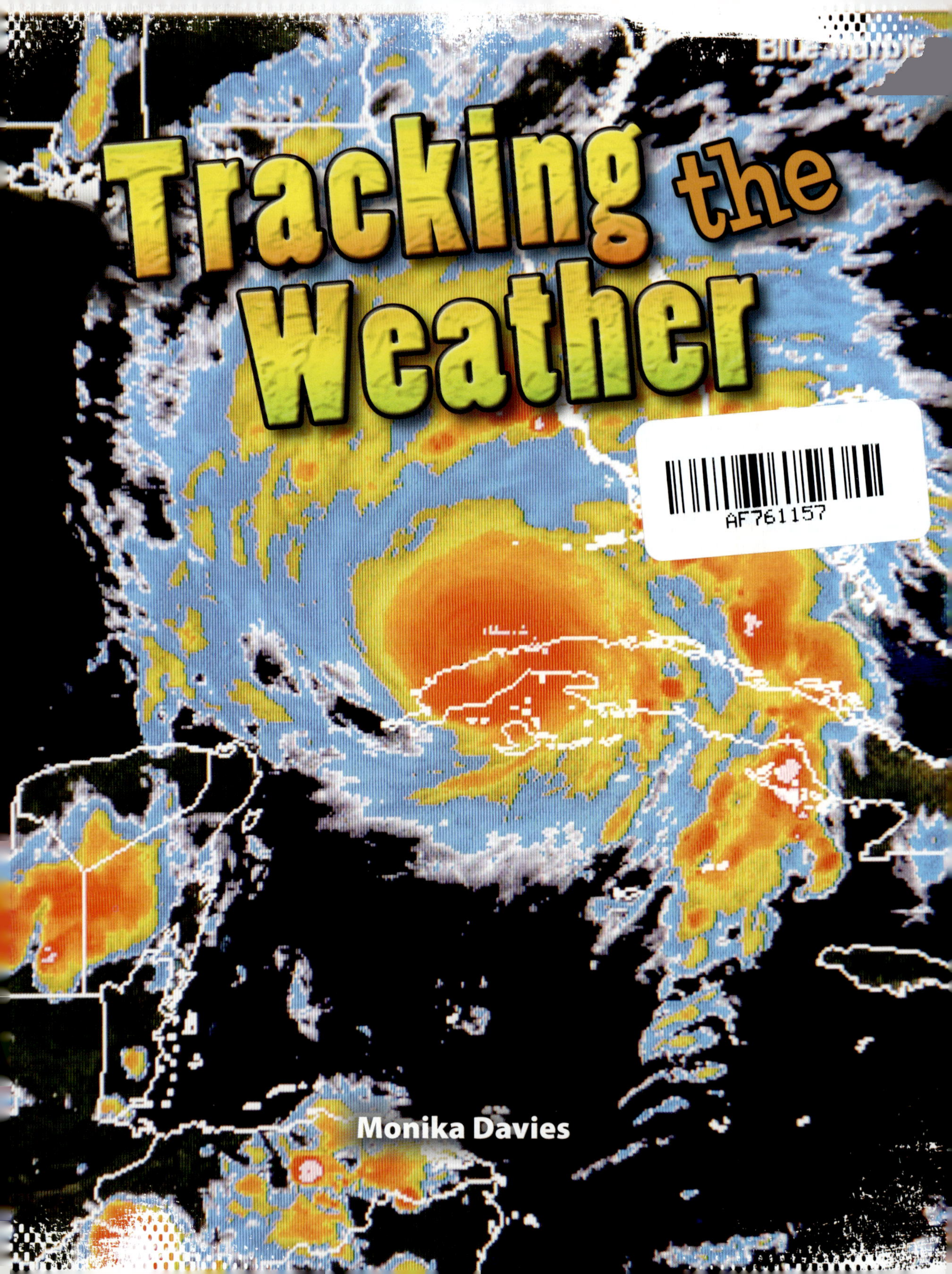

Tracking the Weather

Monika Davies

Consultant

Catherine Hollinger, CID, CLIA
EPA WaterSense Partner
Environmental Consultant

Image Credits: Cover & p.1 dmac/Alamy; p.14 Dennis MacDonald/Alamy; pp.5, 26 Ryan McGinnis/ Alamy; p.9 RGB Ventures/SuperStock/Alamy; p.27 (bottom) ZUMA Press, Inc./Alamy; pp.10, 18, 25 (Illustrations) Tim Bradley; p.11 Cargo Collective; p.12 Lexa Hoang; backcover, pp.6 (background), 10 (left), 14, 15, 20–23 (background), 21 (top & bottom), 24–25 (background), 31 iStock; p.17 STR/ EPA/Newscom; p.4 Getty Images/Science Faction; pp.28–29 (Illustrations) J.J. Rudisill; pp.11, 23 Wikipedia; all other images from Shutterstock.

Library of Congress Cataloging-in-Publication Data

Davies, Monika, author.
Tracking the weather / Monika Davies.
pages cm
Summary: "Rain, sunshine, warm fronts, and cold fronts. Have you ever listened to a weather report? Knowing the weather can help us plan ahead. But reporters aren't the only ones who can track weather. You can, too!"
Audience: K to grade 3.
Includes index.
ISBN 978-1-4807-4648-0 (pbk.)
ISBN 1-4807-4648-7 (pbk.)
ISBN 978-1-4807-5092-0 (ebook)
1. Weather forecasting—Juvenile literature.
2. Meteorological instruments—Juvenile literature.
3. Weather forecasting—Technique—Juvenile literature.
I. Title.
QC995.43.D37 2015
551.63—dc23

2014034278

Teacher Created Materials
5301 Oceanus Drive
Huntington Beach, CA 92649-1030
http://www.tcmpub.com

ISBN 978-1-4807-4648-0

Printed in Malaysia
THU001.48806

Table of Contents

Weather Watchers

Have you looked out the window today? Did you notice if the sun was high in the sky? Or did you see dark rain clouds? Was the wind shaking the trees, or was there snow falling?

Weather is the state of the air at a certain place and time. The sun may be shining. The air may be hot or cold. The wind may be blowing. Or there may be rain falling. These are all different types of weather. Most weather is mild. But some weather is dangerous. **Meteorologists** track the weather so we can predict and plan for changes.

Storm Chasers

Most meteorologists work inside where they and their computers can stay warm and dry. But some meteorologists race outside to catch a glimpse of the latest storms. It is dangerous, but their work helps us better understand how small changes in the air can produce big changes on the ground.

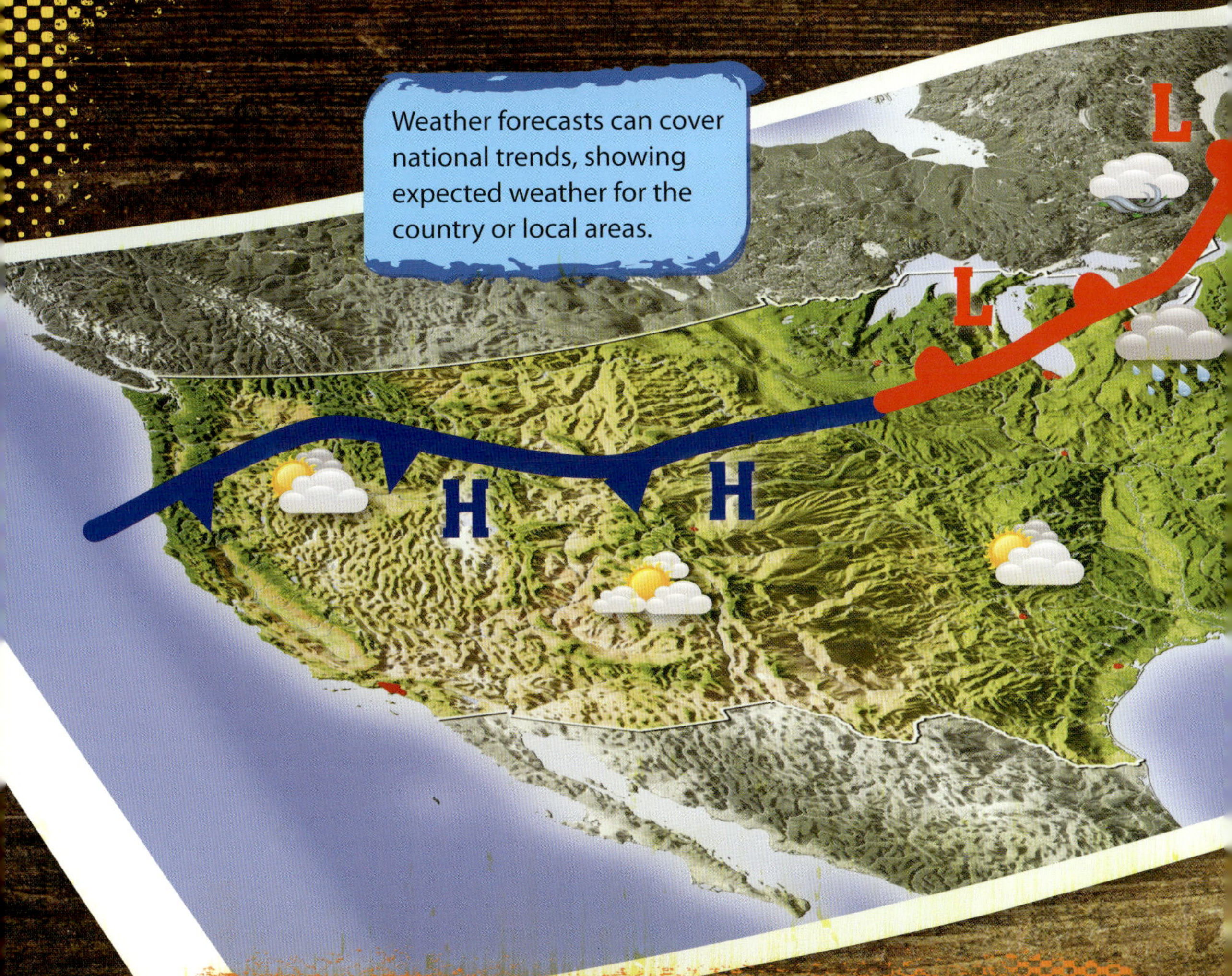

A **forecast** is a prediction of future weather. You can find forecasts in newspapers or online. Simple symbols help readers quickly know what the weather will be. Most forecasts note the high and low **temperatures** expected each day. Checking the forecast can help you prepare for the week. If a storm is coming, you will know to stay inside. If it is going to be sunny, you can plan a day outside.

10:56 PM
Five–Day Forecast
NEW YORK CITY
MONDAY
03:21 PM
High 55°F/13°C
Low 23°F/-5°C
Cloudy, rain, and drizzle into evening
38%
TUESDAY
High 28°F/-2°C
Low 20°F/-7°C
WEDNESDAY
High 46°F/8°C
Low 39°F/4°C
THURSDAY
High 56°F/13°C
Low 36°F/2°C
FRIDAY
High 45°F/7°C
Low 21°F/-6°C
when
where
weather symbol
temperature in Celsius (C) and Fahrenheit (F)

Modern Measurements

Meteorologists use many tools to make their forecasts. Some tools are new and modern. Other tools have been around for hundreds of years. All of them provide powerful **data** for scientists.

Satellites in space take pictures of Earth. They also record data such as wind speed. This information helps experts track weather patterns. These patterns provide clues about weather that is on the way.

Radar tells us where there is water in the air. It can show where the water will fall. Radar can determine if the water will be rain, snow, sleet, or hail.

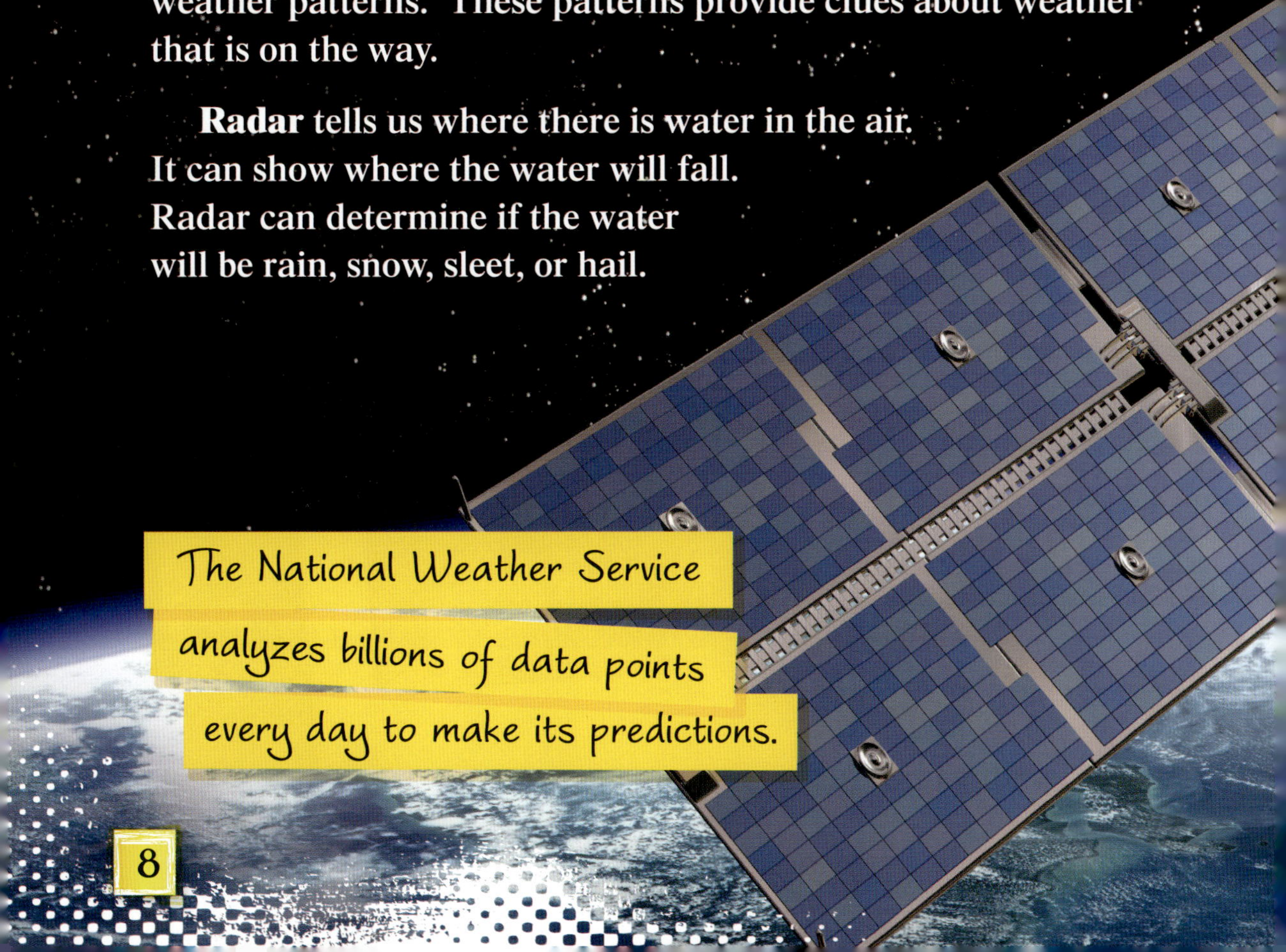

The National Weather Service analyzes billions of data points every day to make its predictions.

A Stormy Surprise

Powerful computers help forecasters make sense of all the data they collect. But weather is constantly changing. And small changes in the weather in one place can affect other areas. That means, sometimes, forecasters get it wrong—and we get a stormy surprise!

Computers use different colors to show the heaviest areas of rain during a storm.

Tracking Temperature

thermometer from the mid-1600s

The first **thermometer** was built in the late 1500s. But this tool is as important as any modern satellite or radar system. Classic thermometers rely on the fact that liquids take up more space when they are warm and less space when they are cold.

If the air is cold, the liquid in a glass thermometer shrinks. If the air is warm, the liquid expands. The top of the liquid always lines up with a number. This number is the temperature. It tells you how hot or cold it is outside. A high number means the weather is very warm. A low number means it is chilly.

Make Your Own Thermometer

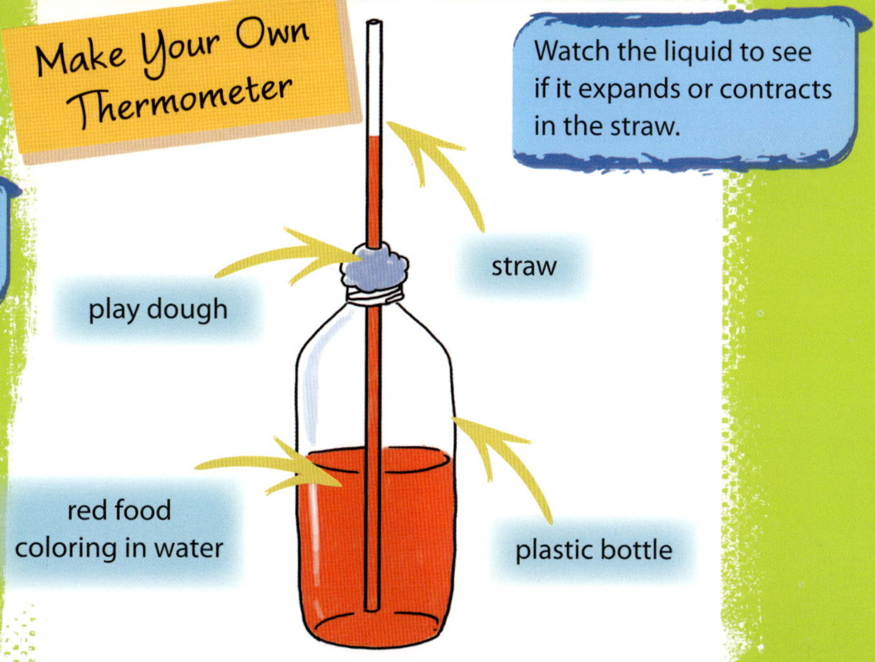

Anders Celsius

Daniel Fahrenheit

The Greek word *metron* means "measure." This root word can be found in the names of many measurement tools.

Meaningful Measurements

Temperature is measured in degrees. There are two ways to measure it—Fahrenheit (°F) and Celsius (°C). Fahrenheit is named after Daniel Fahrenheit. Celsius is named after Anders Celsius. Both methods measure the same thing. But they use different scales—100°F is equal to 38°C.

Scientists track warm and cold fronts in the air. A front is the place where large areas of warm and cold air meet. A cold front occurs where cold air is moving into warm air. It often means rain and thunder are in the forecast. A warm front occurs when warm air moves into a large area of cold air. Warm fronts can cause rain, too. Warm fronts tend to move more slowly than cold fronts.

Extremes

It can get pretty hot on Earth! The hottest day recorded was 58°C (136°F). It can be chilly here, too. The coldest day recorded was -92°C (-134°F).

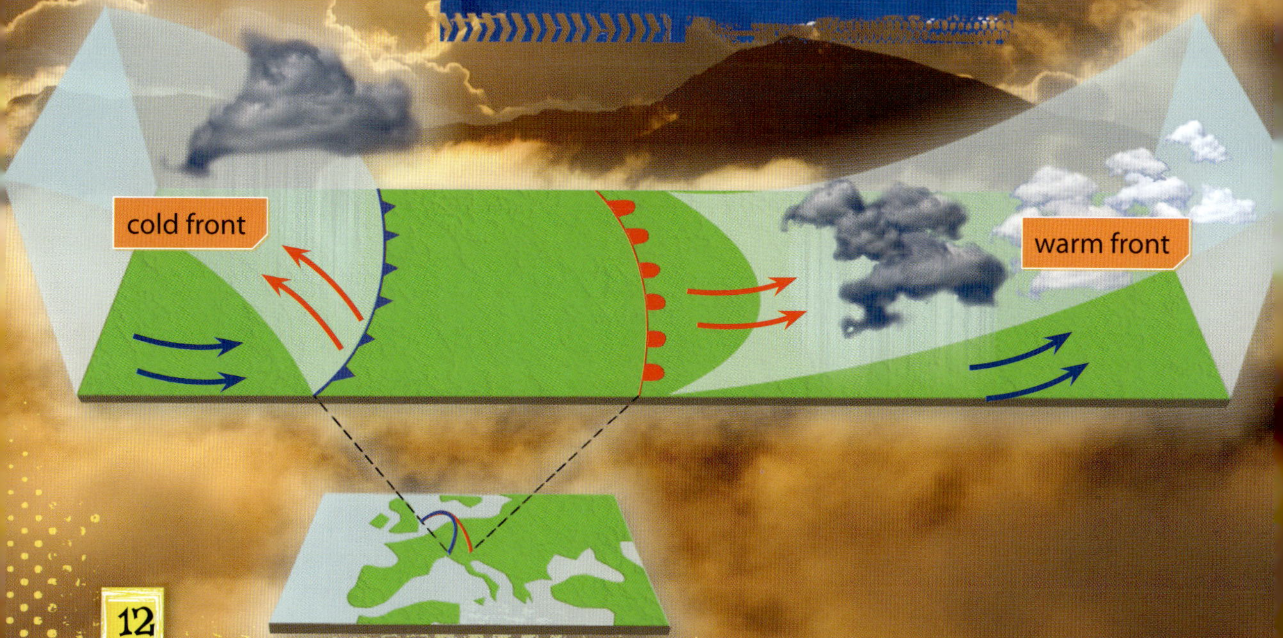

This scale shows the temperature in degrees Fahrenheit.

Seasonal Temperatures

Temperatures change where we live every day. We can use bar graphs to record these changes. Each graph below shows the weekly average temperature for a town.

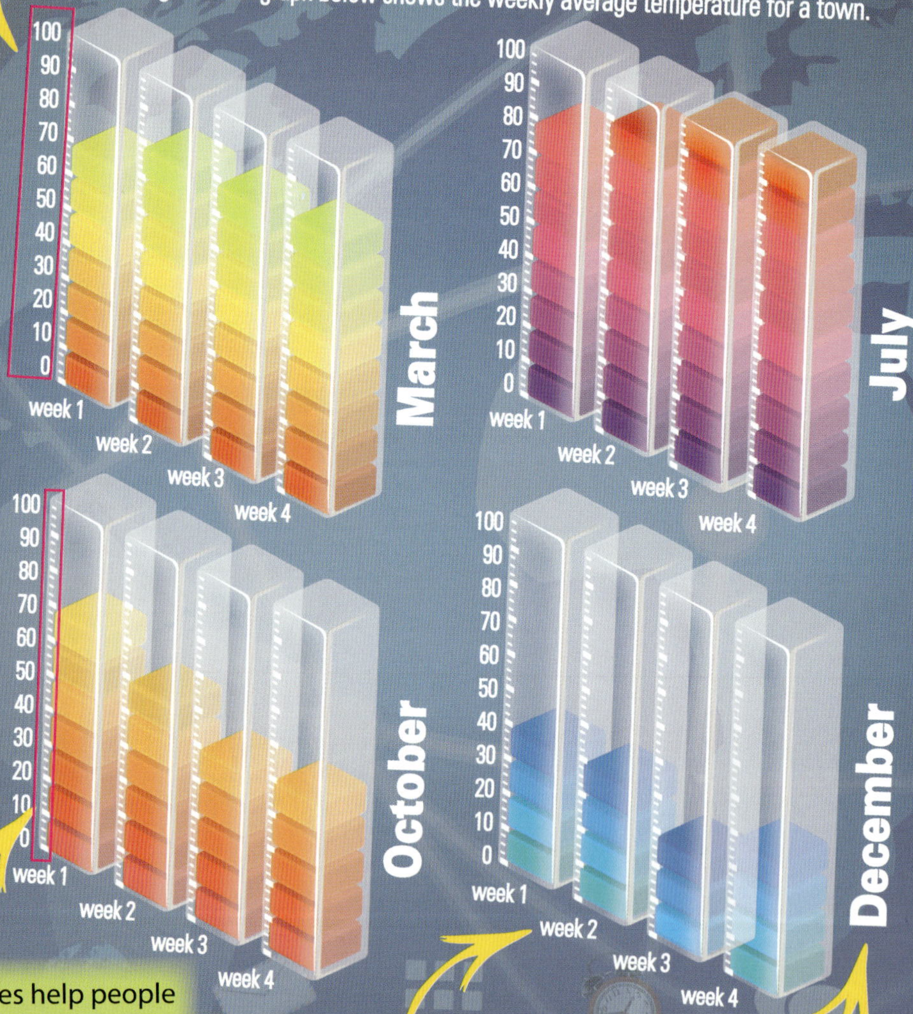

Grid lines help people read the data.

Labels show the category (month) being measured (in weeks).

Recording the Rain

If you see dark clouds low in the sky, grab your umbrella or run inside. These are stratus clouds, and they are full of rain! A large storm can do more than soak your clothes. It can damage power lines and cause flooding.

Scientists use radar to predict when and where rain will strike. News reports show the path a storm is expected to take. They tell the **probability** of a storm hitting nearby areas.

Forecasters create special maps to help people understand when and where a storm will hit. The numbers in the icons show how powerful the hurricane will be in each location.

Cloud Chart

Clouds in the sky can provide clues about what the weather will be. There are many types of clouds. These are some of the most common.

Stratus clouds are flat and long. Rain is probably in the forecast when these clouds are low and gray.

Cirrus (SIR-uhs) clouds look like wispy feathers high in the sky. Warm days are most likely ahead when these clouds arrive.

Cumulus clouds are puffy and often low in the sky. They can grow very tall. These clouds can be seen on a sunny day. But, sometimes they produce serious storms.

Clouds are made of tiny water droplets.

Scientists track rain as it approaches. Then, once it arrives, they measure it. A **rain gauge** is an instrument that shows how much rain has fallen. An open container with numbered lines on the side catches rain when it falls. The lines show how much liquid is in the container.

If you want to use a rain gauge during a big storm, place it outside in an open area. Avoid placing it by trees or bushes. (They could affect the amount of water that drops into the gauge.) When the storm is over, the gauge will show how much rain fell from the sky.

The Raindrop Report

We can track how much rain has fallen with a pictograph. This graph shows one rainy week with sections for each day. Each section has a number of raindrops. A raindrop represents half an inch of rain. Can you tell which day had the most rain? If you said Wednesday, you are right!

Meghalaya, India, receives the most inches of rain per year. The name Meghalaya means "land of the clouds."

Assessing Air Pressure

We may say something is as "light as air." But scientists know air can be heavy. Air in the **atmosphere** pushes down on us all the time, and this pressure has a big effect on weather.

A **barometer** measures air pressure. Barometers are made of a glass tube and are filled with liquid. The bottom of the tube is open and sits inside the cup.

Make Your Own Barometer

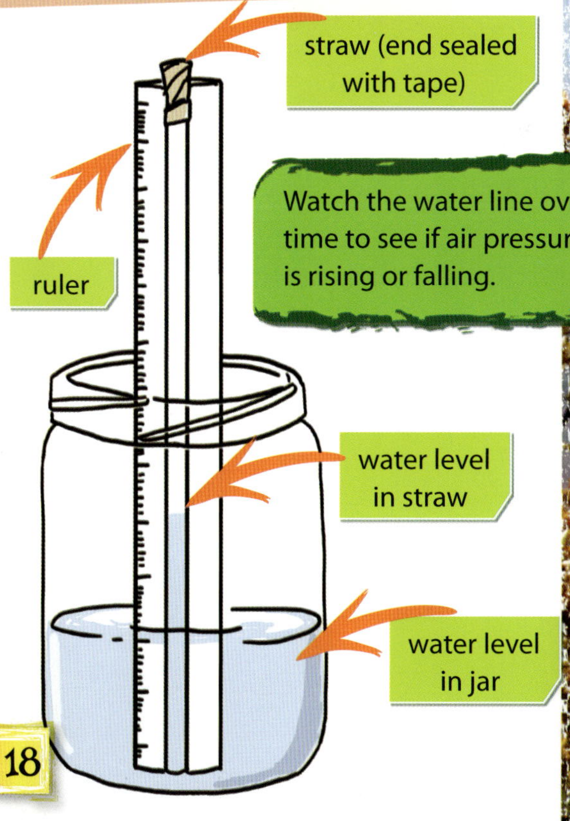

Under Pressure

The atmosphere presses down on every square inch of Earth—and you—with one kilogram per square centimeter of force. The air inside your body balances this pressure and prevents you from being crushed.

Air pressure decreases where the atmosphere is thinner—like at the top of a mountain!

When air pressure is high, air pushes down on the liquid in the cup. The liquid inside the tube is then pushed up. When air pressure is low, air does not push down as hard. The liquid inside the tube goes down.

Scientists use barometers to measure air pressure. If air pressure is high, air is sinking. When air sinks closer to Earth, it becomes dry. Dry air means there will likely be sunny skies.

If air pressure is low, air is rising. When air rises away from Earth, it changes into clouds and rain. Wet air can cause stormy weather.

Watch your barometer closely. The higher the number, the higher the pressure. If air pressure is high, you will likely see clear skies. If air pressure is low, it may be time to put on your rain boots.

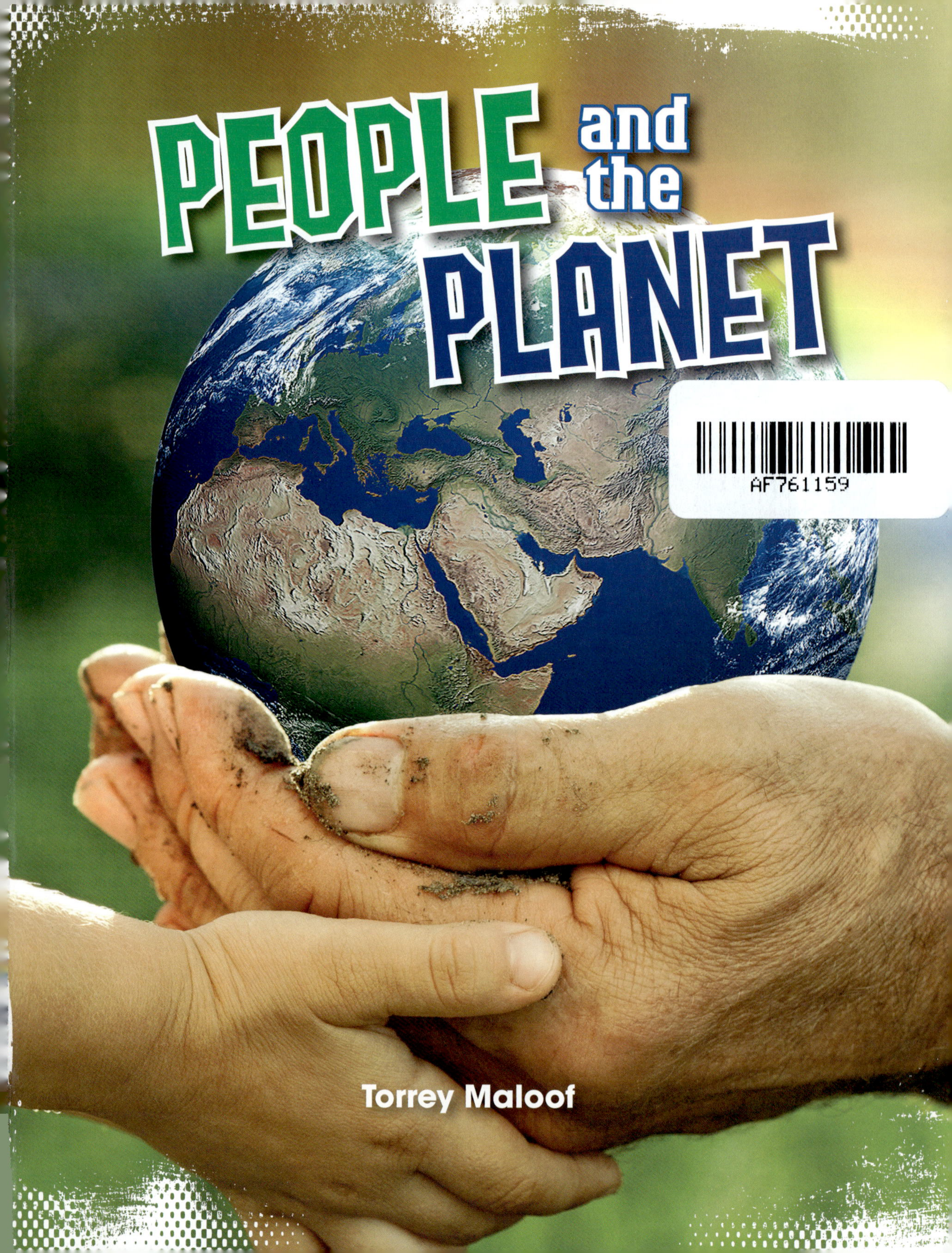

PEOPLE and the PLANET

Torrey Maloof

Consultant

Catherine Hollinger, CID, CLIA
EPA WaterSense Partner
Environmental Consultant

Image Credits: p.27 (bottom) Ambient Images Inc./Alamy; p.5 (top) Frances Roberts/Alamy; pp.14–15 (background) James Osmond/Alamy; p.11 (bottom left) Premium Stock Photography GmbH/ Alamy; p.11 (top) Stephen Dorey ABIPP/Alamy; p.17 (illustration) Tim Bradley; pp.5 (bottom), 7 (top), 8–9 (background), 10 (top left), 11 (background), 16–17 (background), 18–19, 21 (bottom right), 22–23 (background), 24–25 (background), 26–27 (background), 30 iStock; p.12 (left) AFP/Getty Images/Newscom; pp.12–13 (background) NHPA/ Photoshot/Newscom; pp.2–3, 31 Ton Koene/VWPics/ Newscom; pp.6–7 Rob Blakers; p.25 (top) Jason Lin/ Project TGIF; p.32 Ken Lax/Science Source; p.10 (bottom left) Martin Harvey/Science Source; p.10 (right) Nigel J. Dennis/Science Source; pp.28–29 (illustrations) J.J. Rudisill; all other images from Shutterstock.

Library of Congress Cataloging-in-Publication Data

Maloof, Torrey, author.
People and the planet / Torrey Maloof.
pages cm
Summary: "We live on planet Earth. It gives us the things we need to survive. When it changes, it affects us all. But humans also affect Earth, and it's changing the planet we call home. It's important that we take care of our planet so it can continue to take care of us."-- Provided by publisher.
Audience: K to grade 3.
Includes index.
ISBN 978-1-4807-4650-3 (pbk.)
ISBN 978-1-4807-5094-4 (ebook)
1. Human ecology--Juvenile literature.
2. Nature—Effect of human beings on—Juvenile literature.
3. Environmental protection—Juvenile literature. I. Title.
GF48.M35 2015
304.2'8—dc23

2014034281

Teacher Created Materials
5301 Oceanus Drive
Huntington Beach, CA 92649-1030
http://www.tcmpub.com

ISBN 978-1-4807-4650-3

Printed in China
YiCai.032019.CA201901471

Table of Contents

Our Changing Planet

Imagine that each day you came home and found more people living in your house. What if they left trash lying around the house? What if they ate all the food in your kitchen? What if they started pulling boards out of the wall to build furniture? What if they burned the house down trying to stay warm? And what if billions of people around the world were all living this way?

The way we live does affect our home—Earth. Over time, our presence on Earth has changed it. Every day, we use its **natural resources**. We use the planet's water to grow our food. We use its oil to make fuel. We change the landscape of Earth's surface. We farm the land. We cut down forests to build homes. We change Earth's **atmosphere** with harmful substances released by cars and factories.

Scientists are learning that all these changes have serious consequences. People have lived on Earth for a long time. But we are just beginning to see the impact of our actions on our planet. We need to use its resources carefully. We need to make wise choices that will protect our planet.

Saving the Planet

Conservationists are people who work to protect land, plants, and animals. Conservationists find ways to conserve our natural resources.

The Earth is the only home we have.
We must work together to protect it.

Deforestation

One way people change the planet is by cutting down and removing trees from forests. This is called *deforestation*. There are many reasons trees are cut down. Trees are a natural resource. People cut down trees to use the wood to make paper and build homes. Wood can also be used to heat homes or cook food. The demand for wood and paper is high. So more forests are being cut down every day.

Some people clear forests to make room for crops. But after a few years, the soil may lose its **nutrients**. It's not as rich without trees. This makes it difficult for crops to grow there.

Disappearing Forests

Deforestation is occurring in all of the biggest rainforests around the world. The countries with the most serious deforestation problems are Brazil, Malaysia, and Nepal.

"At first I thought I was fighting to save rubber trees, then I thought I was fighting to save the Amazon rainforest. Now I realize I am fighting for humanity."
—Chico Mendes, conservationist

Deforestation is changing the entire planet. Seventy percent of land animals live in forests. When forests are cut down, these animals lose their homes. They may even become extinct, or die out. This can happen to plants, too.

Land **erosion** is also a problem. Tree roots hold soil in place. But when trees are cut down, soil loosens. This allows wind and water to wear away the land. The soil that is left will no longer absorb water. Instead, water rushes over it. This causes floods and landslides.

Trees also help us breathe. They do this by turning **carbon dioxide** into oxygen. We need oxygen to breathe. When forests are cut down, less oxygen is made. And there is more carbon dioxide in the air. This increases the **greenhouse effect**.

Planting new trees is one way to prevent deforestation.

The Consequences of Deforestation

Forests the size of Panama are being cut down every year. The consequences, such as floods and landslides, are dramatic.

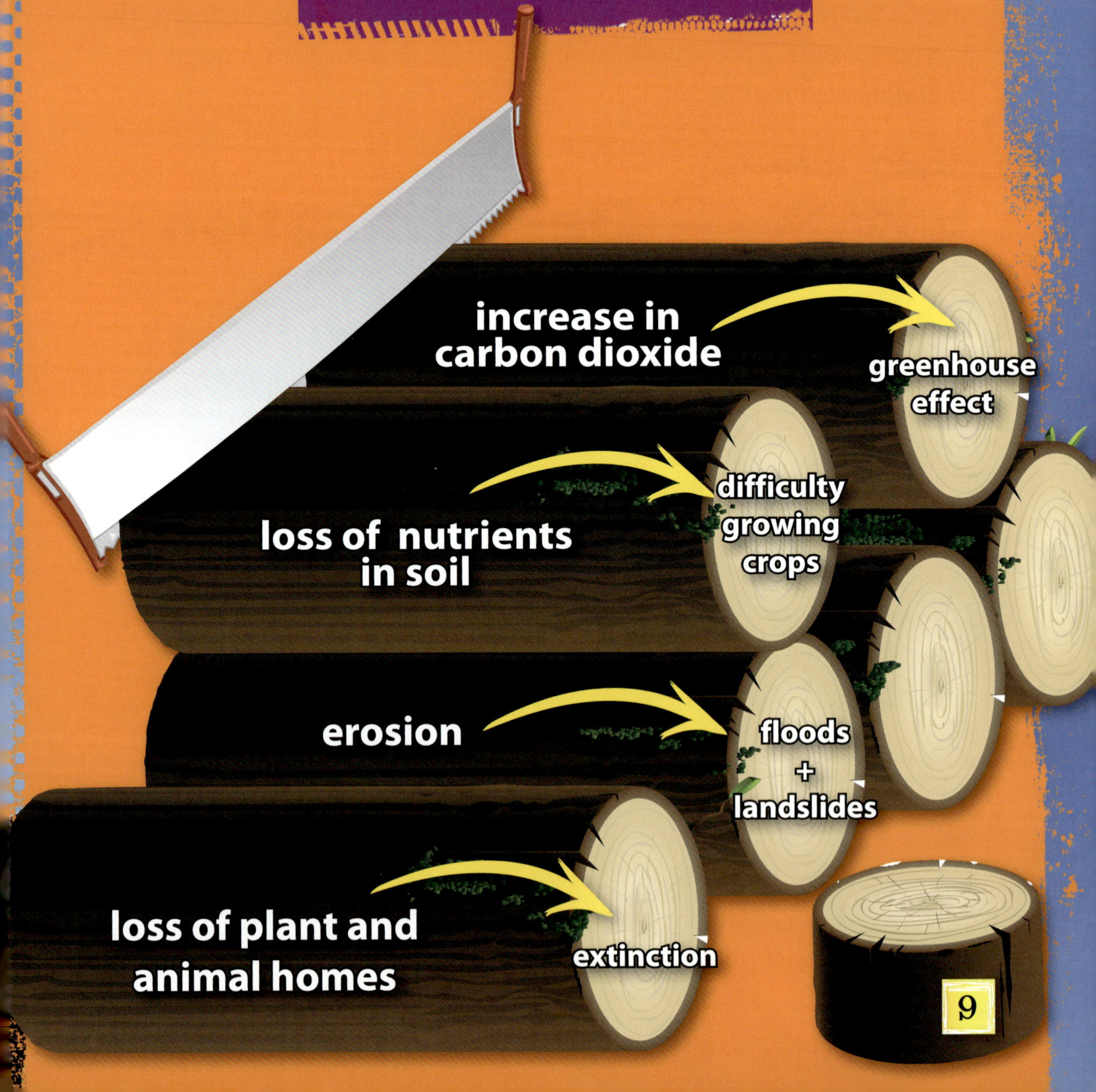

Desertification

The land on Earth is limited. We use this land for shelter and food. But sometimes, we overuse the land. We cut down too many trees. We pull too much water from the soil. When this happens, the land dries out. Soon, it can turn into a true desert. This process is called *desertification*.

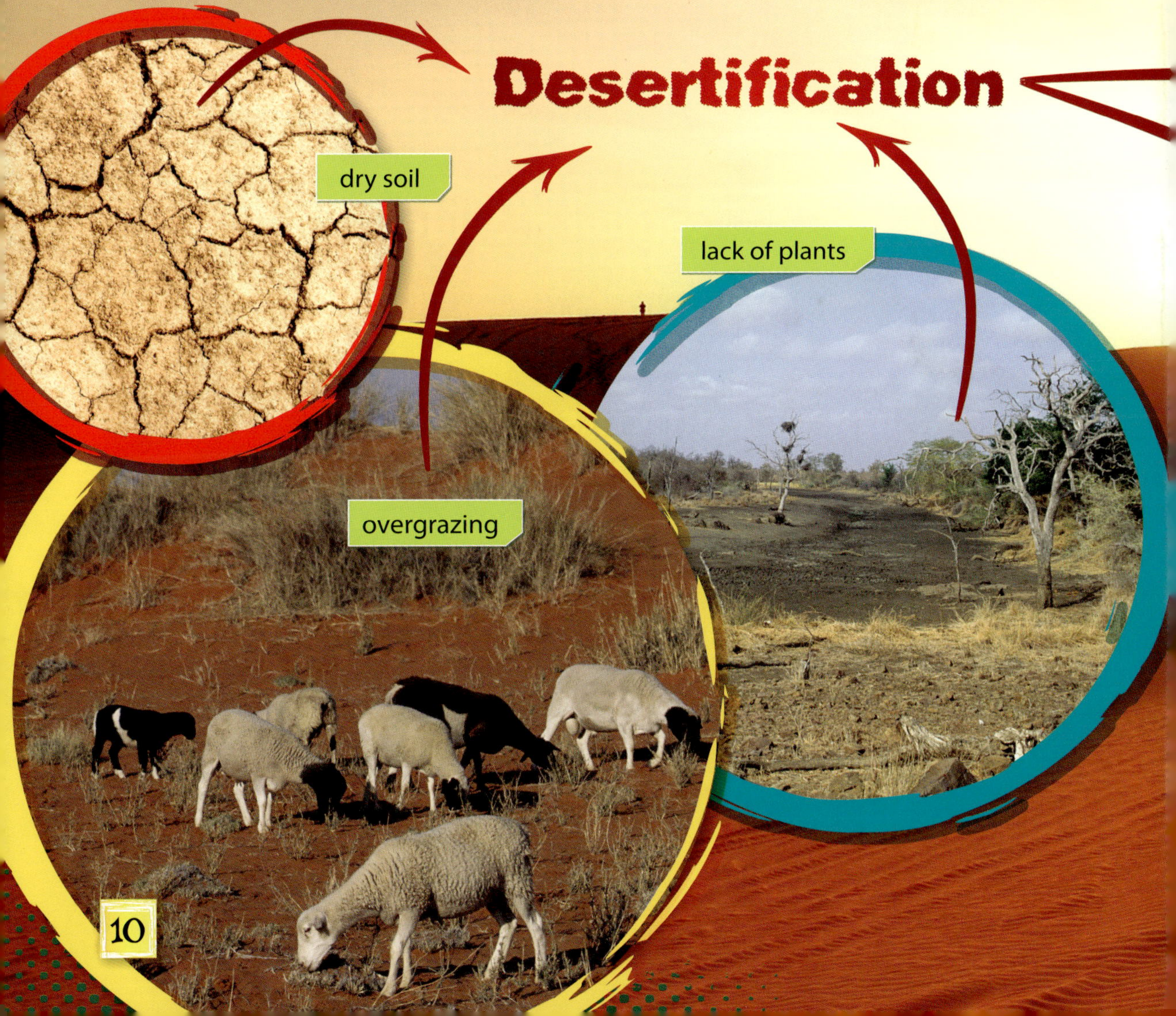

Desertification is a natural process. It occurs by itself over time. But lately, humans have sped up the process. Today, it is happening all over the world. And it is happening quickly. The problem is more serious in areas with lots of people and a dry **climate**. These areas grow many crops. They also raise large numbers of animals. They do this to make sure there is enough food for everyone. But over time, this causes problems.

Spreading South

There are two areas that are seriously suffering from desertification. One area is south of the Sahara Desert in Africa. The other area is south of the Gobi Desert in China.

Crops pull a lot of water and nutrients from soil. When an area does not get enough rain, soil becomes even drier. Soon, crops die. At the same time, farm animals graze on nearby plants. They can eat so many plants that the land grows bare. When crops die and there are no other plants left, soil loosens. This makes the land wear away quickly. The land becomes more desert-like.

More Trees, Please

Wangari Maathai (won-GAHR-ee muh-TAHY) hated seeing the effects of desertification near her home in Kenya. So, she worked with others to plant millions of trees. The trees helped prevent desertification. In 2004, she won a Nobel Peace Prize for her work.

One of the biggest problems of desertification is famine (FAM-in). Many people in these places do not have enough food to eat. And as more land turns to desert, there will not be enough good soil to grow crops.

Desertification also causes **droughts**. These long periods of dry weather make it even harder for plants and animals to survive. Some people must walk great distances to find drinking water. With little rain, the cycle continues and deserts grow larger.

A single cow can eat 18 kilograms (40 pounds) of food per day.

Pollution

It's not just the things we do directly to the land that change the planet. There are many things we do to make our lives easier and more fun that also damage the planet. We use electricity to light our homes at night. It helps us read when it is dark outside or play video games when it rains. Planes help us travel farther. They take us to faraway places for fabulous vacations. Cars help us go faster. They get us to school quickly or to a baseball game on time. We can take clean water with us everywhere we go thanks to plastic water bottles. These things help us and make life more enjoyable. But they also have a big impact on our planet.

Pollution is the process of making land, air, or water dirty and unsafe. Factories that make power often pollute the air. Cars and planes pollute the air, too. And plastic water bottles pollute the land.

Eliminating e-Waste

Digital or electronic devices such as TVs, batteries, or MP3 players can harm the environment when people dispose of them incorrectly. E-waste can leak dangerous chemicals into the ground and water. Cities often collect this waste on special days to help prevent pollution.

In one year, Americans use more than 50 billion plastic water bottles!

Every year, the number of people in the world rises. More people means more pollution. It means more trash ends up in our landfills. More toxic smoke enters the air. More **hazardous** waste mixes with our water. Pollution affects our planet in many ways, none of which are good. Today, pollution is a problem all around the world.

All living things need clean air to breathe and survive. Burning fossil fuels makes our air dirty. Factories burn fuel. We burn fuel when we use cars, trains, and planes. All of these things produce smoke, which pollutes the air with chemicals. The chemicals enter the atmosphere and mix with the rain. This polluted rain is called *acid rain*. Acid rain pollutes the ground and water. The water becomes harmful. This polluted water can damage plants and animals. It can also make humans sick.

Try walking with a friend instead of driving somewhere to save fossil fuels.

Fossil Fuels

Coal, oil, and natural gas are fossil fuels. Fossil fuels are found in rocks deep in the ground. They take millions of years to make. They are made from the remains of dead plants and animals.

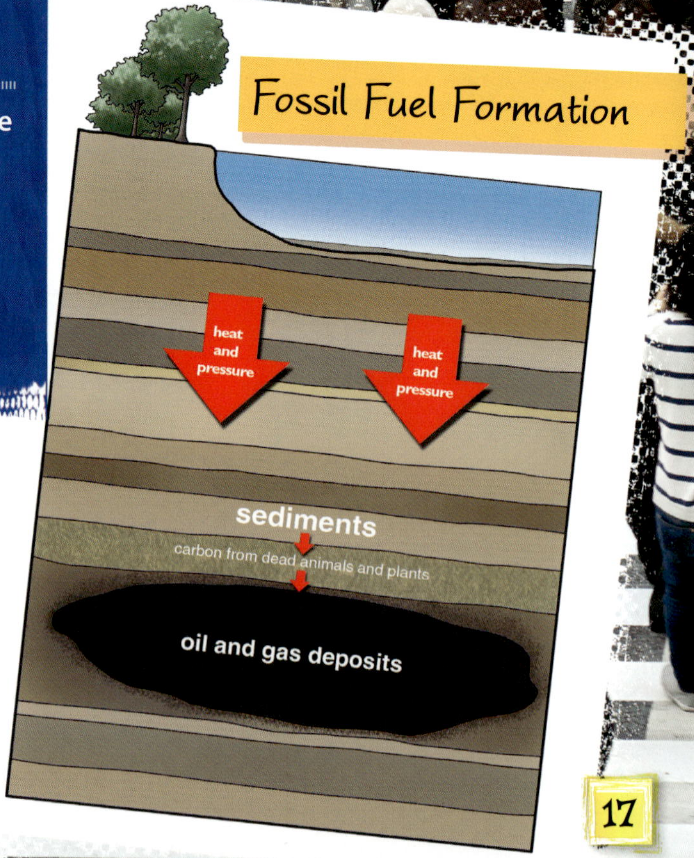

The greenhouse effect is a natural process. But humans speed up the process by polluting the air. It is natural for carbon dioxide to be in the air. People and animals breathe it out. Carbon dioxide traps heat on Earth. Some of the heat escapes into space. Some heat returns to Earth. Just the right amount of heat helps keep our planet warm.

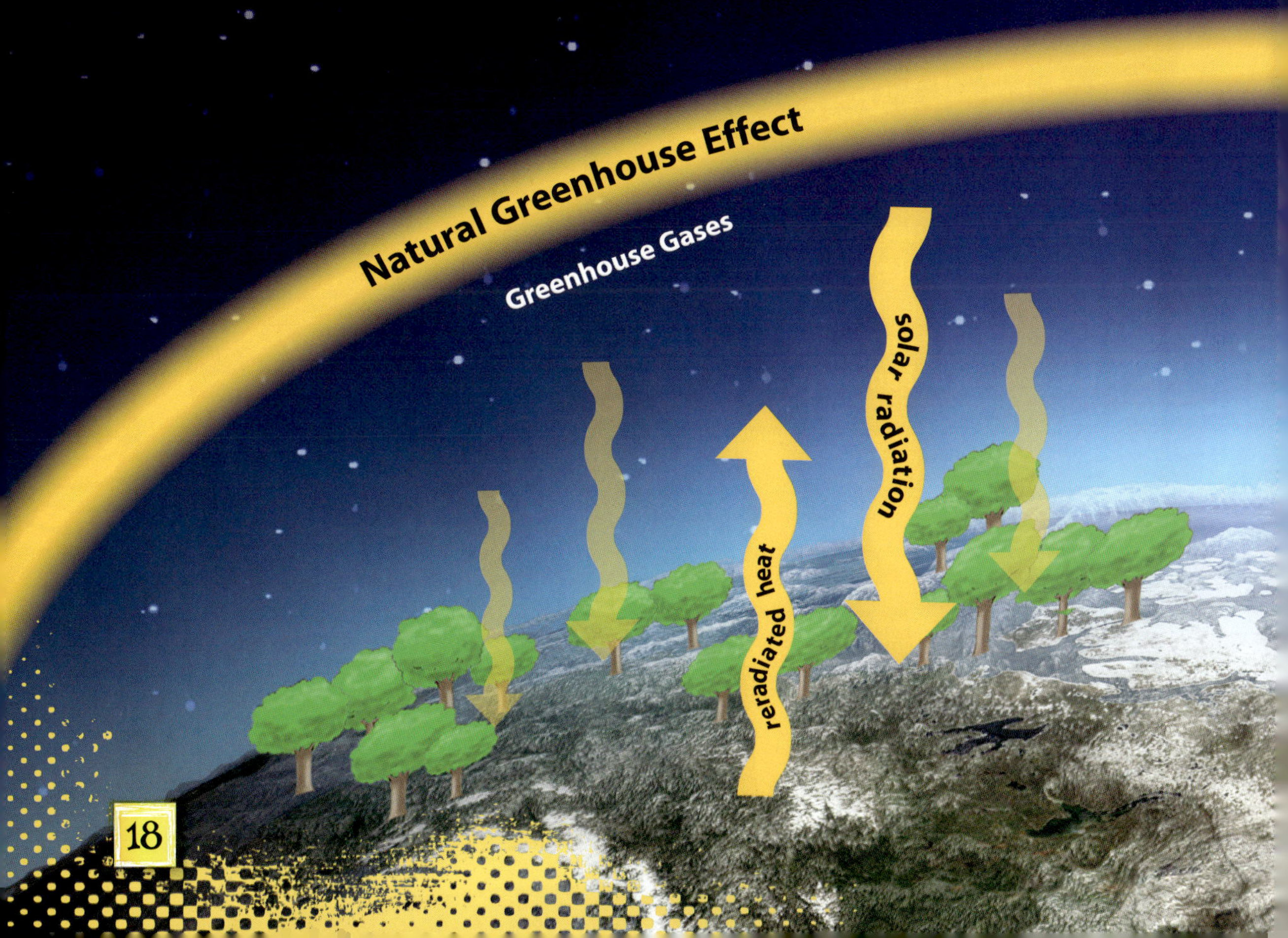

But when people burn fossil fuels, too much carbon dioxide is released into the air too quickly. When there is too much carbon dioxide in the air, too much heat gets trapped. This causes problems. Too much trapped heat can cause Earth's overall temperature to rise. This is known as *global warming*.

Harsh Changes

Scientists think global warming is responsible for these and other changes in the environment:

- higher temperatures
- intense weather
- more droughts
- shrinking sea ice

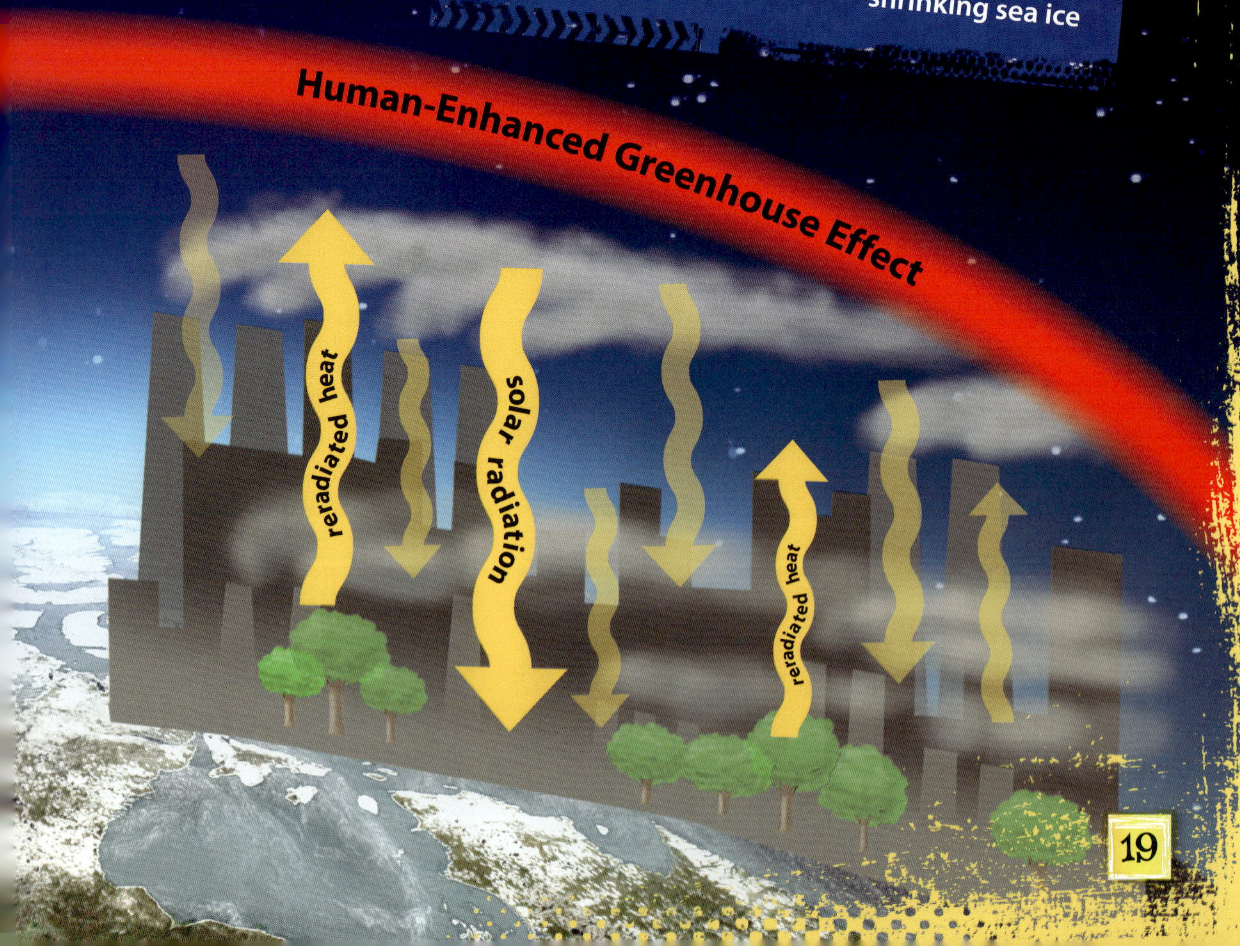

Terracing

People change the environment in many ways. But not all of them are bad. Terraces are large flat areas on hills or the sides of mountains. Building them is a simple, but powerful way to change the land.

In East and Southeast Asia, rice is an important part of nearly every meal. Rice is more nutritious than other grains, such as wheat. Rice has **carbohydrates**, which provide us with energy. However, growing rice is not easy. It requires a lot of hard work. But a small number of rice fields can feed a large number of people. Most of East and Southeast Asia consists of hills or mountains. This is not ideal farmland. To make it easier to grow crops, people have created terraces.

A farmer plants rice.

Thoughtful Farming

Terraces are used all across the world to grow many different things.

Terraces look like a series of steps carved into the land. They are mainly used for crops that need a lot of water, such as rice. Rice is grown in paddies, or flooded fields. Farmers must control the flow of water to grow rice. Terraces can help do this. If the paddies were on mountains without terraces, the water would just wash away. This would leave the rice shoots too dry to grow. Terracing changes the physical landscape of Earth. But it changes it in a good way. Terraces help hold rainwater. They keep the water from rushing downhill. This helps slow down erosion. It also helps to stop landslides and floods. Terraces also create farmland in areas that are not fit for farming. This helps to feed many people in areas where it is difficult to grow food.

Timeless Terraces

There are rice terraces in the Philippines that are more than 2,000 years old! They are the Banaue (BUH-now-ee) Rice Terraces. They cover more than 10,360 square kilometers (4,000 square miles) of land.

Rice comes in many colors and varieties.

Saving Our Planet

Our planet will stay the same size. It will not grow any larger. But every year, more and more people are living on Earth. The human family is growing in size. But our home is not. Experts wonder where everyone will live. Will there be enough food for everyone? What will we do with all of our trash? We depend on the planet for our survival. And the planet's survival depends on us.

Some people are finding new ways for us to live on Earth. They are called **environmentalists**. They have many ideas for how we can save our planet. They help farmers come up with new ways to grow crops and raise animals. They are finding ways to slow desertification. They teach people different ways to decrease pollution. They are also showing people why it is good to use natural forms of energy, such as wind or solar power.

Do Something

In 2008, fifth-grader Cassandra Lin started the project Turn Grease Into Fuel. She worked with other kids to collect cooking oil from local restaurants. They passed it on to families to use as inexpensive fuel for heating. The group has prevented more than two million pounds of carbon dioxide from entering the air.

You can help save our planet, too! You can reduce the amount of trash you make. Drink from glasses instead of plastic water bottles. Use boxes or fabric bags instead of plastic bags when you go shopping. And, you can recycle!

You can also turn off lights when they are not in use. This saves energy. You can ride your bike or walk to school. This helps reduce air pollution. You can also use less electricity by putting on a sweater instead of turning on a heater. These may seem like little things. But all these little things make a big difference.

We are still learning how to make the best use of the world we live in. What we have learned is that we need to take care of Earth because it takes care of us.

"It's the little things citizens do.
That's what will make the difference.
My little thing is planting trees."
—Wangari Maathai, conservationist

Think Like a Scientist

How do trees prevent soil erosion? Experiment and find out!

What to Get

- damp sand
- small block
- tray
- twigs and grass
- water

What to Do

1. Pack damp sand into a shallow tray. Make sure the sand is level.

2. Prop one end of the tray up on a block.

3. Carve out a curvy line in the sand with your finger. Place twigs and grass along the line to represent trees.

4. Slowly pour water into the higher end of the line.

5. Record what happens as the water flows down the line. Note where erosion occurs and where it is avoided.

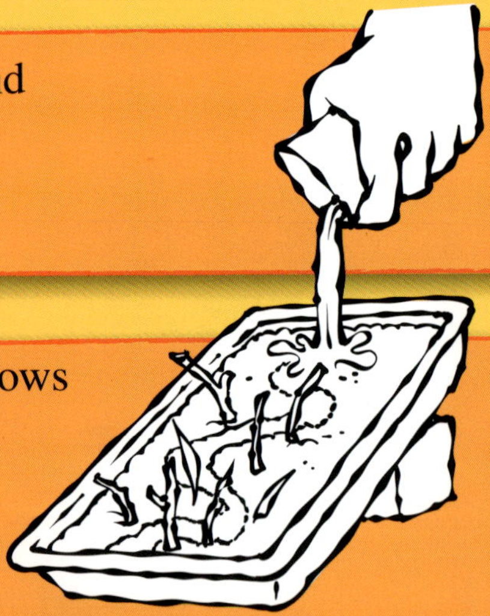

Glossary

atmosphere—the mass of air that surrounds Earth

carbohydrates—substances found in foods such as bread, rice, and potatoes which provide the human body with heat and energy

carbon dioxide—a gas that is produced when people and animals breathe out

climate—the usual type of weather a place gets

droughts—long periods of time with little or no rain

environmentalists—people who work to protect Earth from pollution and other threats

erosion—the process by which something wears away by natural forces such as water, wind, or ice

greenhouse effect—the natural warming of Earth's atmosphere

hazardous—dangerous or risky

natural resources—things existing in the natural world such as wood, oil, or minerals

nutrients—substances that living things need to live and grow

Index

Your Turn!

Help Our Planet

It's important that we take care of Earth because it takes care of us. Make a poster listing 10 things your community is doing to help save the environment. Share your findings with friends and family. Everyone can make a difference—including you!

Zeroth Law

There are four laws of thermodynamics. There is a first, second, third, and zeroth law. The zeroth law was added after the others. It was more basic than the others, so it needed to have a number that came before one. People thought it was obvious, but still important. The zeroth law says that heat only goes from hot things to cooler things.

Marie Curie

Marie Curie (1867–1934) was born Marie Sklodowska in Poland. During her time, it was rare for women to study science and math. But that is just what she did. And like many other women scientists of her time, she married a scientist. In that way, she was allowed to continue her work. Women who lived during that time usually weren't given the means to do the work without a man present. Fortunately, times have changed a great deal since then.

It's a good thing for science that Curie kept going! She won two Nobel Prizes: one for physics in 1903, and the other for chemistry in 1911. The Nobel Prize is a top honor for a scientist whose work changes or advances science in a big way. Marie Curie's work certainly did.

Marie Curie

Seeing in the Dark

Objects give off heat radiation. This is why infrared cameras can be used to see things in the dark. They see the heat. Objects that give off the most heat show up best when infrared sensors are used.

Heat moves in three ways. They are **conduction**, **convection**, and **radiation**. Conduction happens when vibrating atoms pass heat to each other. Convection happens when warm material moves to a cooler area and takes heat with it. Radiation happens when energy moves in rays or waves.

In Planck's time, people knew about the first two types of heat movement. But they didn't know much about the third. Planck explained what radiation is. For example, the light and heat we get from the sun is made of radiation waves.

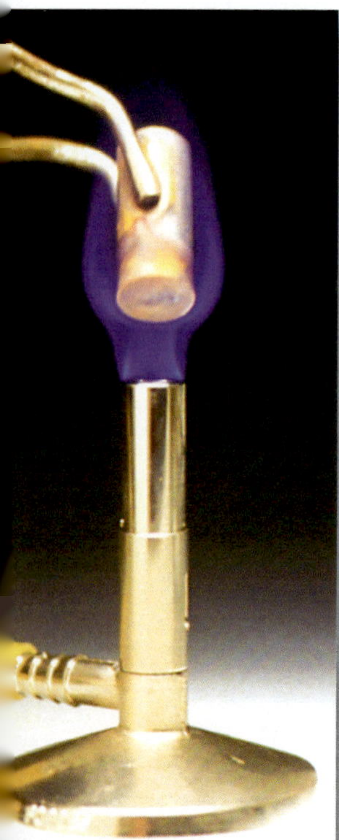

conduction

convection

radiation

Entropy

To understand heat, Planck needed to know more than just how it moves. One of the most important things he studied is called **entropy** (EN-truh-pee). It is an idea that was very useful to Planck. It became an important part of his own ideas.

Entropy is the messiness or randomness in a system. In a system with high entropy, the atoms are very disordered. This is something like a messy bedroom. If all your belongings are thrown all over your room, there is high entropy there, and no order. In other words, there is a high level of randomness.

In a system with low entropy, atoms are orderly. This is like a bedroom that has just been tidied. Everything is in a place that makes sense. Clothes are in the closet. Books are stacked neatly on the shelves. Things are in order. There is low entropy. In other words, there is a low level of randomness.

What a Mess!

The second law of thermodynamics says that heat and energy will move around until things are as disordered as possible.

Heat Death of the Universe

If there is only a certain amount of energy in the universe, and nothing can come in or out of the universe, and entropy increases all the time, then there should be a point where entropy is as high as it can get. At this point, the universe would be a complete mess. There would be no more movement. There would be no energy to make anything do what it is supposed to do. This point is called the heat death of the universe. Scientists don't know if it will actually happen. They don't know because nobody knows if there is anything outside the universe.

The Energy in Light

Light is a wave. It carries energy. Different colors of light have different energies. Planck showed how to figure the energy carried by colors of light. He did this by linking light waves to entropy.

Stephen Hawking

Stephen Hawking was born in England in 1942. He has been a student of physics since he was young. For many years, he has been a famous physics researcher and college professor.

Hawking holds a post of great honor at Cambridge University. The post is called the Lucasian Professor of Mathematics. It was founded in 1663. In 1669, it was given to the great scientist and mathematician, Isaac Newton. Hawking follows in his footsteps.

Hawking is also known for his physical disability. He has a disease called ALS, which severely restricts his speech and movement. He communicates with a special device that can either print or speak his words. His only regret is that the device has an American accent!

Hawking says that he has led a fairly normal life. He is married and has children and grandchildren. And he has spent many years doing work that he loves.

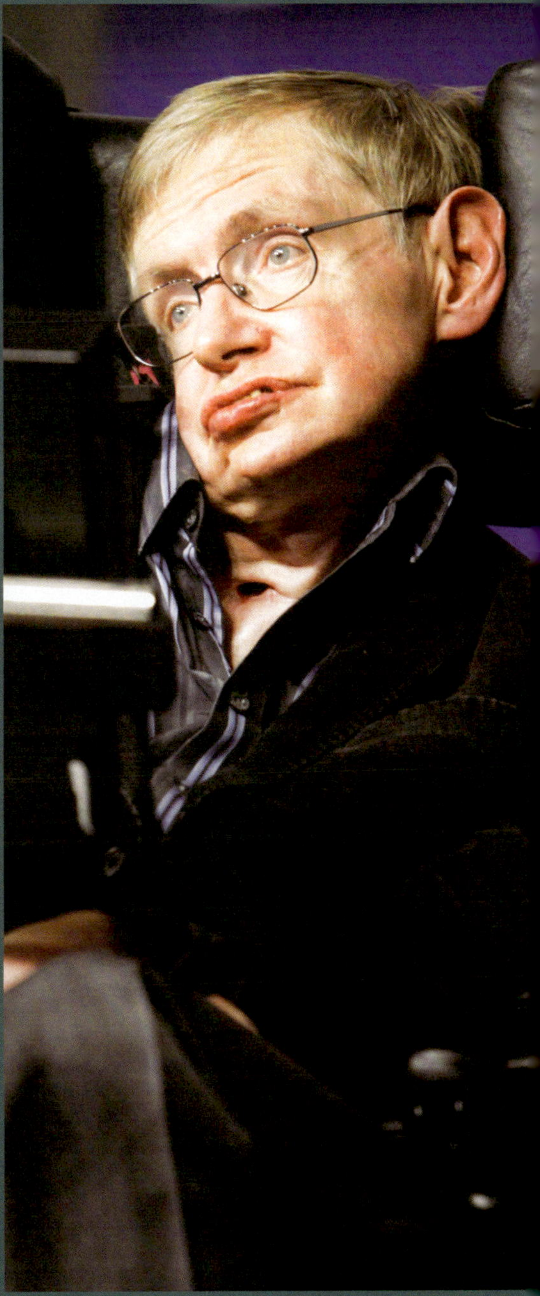

Another example of a low-entropy system is a new deck of playing cards. The cards are in suit and number order. After they are shuffled, they are in random order. This is like a high-entropy system.

When entropy goes up, things become more and more disordered. This is like the bedroom that hasn't been tidied in a while. Things just seem to continue to get out of order. They become more and more random.

For that to change, a lot of energy needs to be put in. This is just like the effort needed to tidy a very messy bedroom. The more random the mess, the more energy it takes to clean it up.

"h"

Planck is famous for a very important formula. The formula contains "Planck's Constant," or "h." It is part of his theory on light and energy. The constant can be found on Planck's tombstone in Germany. It reads: $h = 6.626 \times 10^{-34}$ Joules seconds (J s)

Two decks of playing cards: one arranged in order and one shuffled up with entropy.

Quantum Theory

Planck's study of entropy led him to a new idea. It became an important theory. It tells about energy and the world of atoms.

For years, the laws of physics were clear. They explained what people wanted to know. But they didn't explain the movement inside of atoms. **Quantum** (KWON-tuhm) theory did.

Planck said that energy comes in tiny packets called **quanta** (KWON-tuh). One quanta is a quantum. Quanta move in their own ways. This explains many things. For example, it explains the way electrons move. Electrons are small particles inside atoms. It also explains why some things are radioactive. **Radioactivity** happens when the nucleus, or core, of some atoms breaks down. Those atoms release energy.

Quantum theory was Planck's greatest success. It changed the way scientists understood the world.

Scientists have used quantum theory to "teleport" information from one place to another instantly. Someday you won't have to wait for a webpage to load: It will teleport right to your screen!

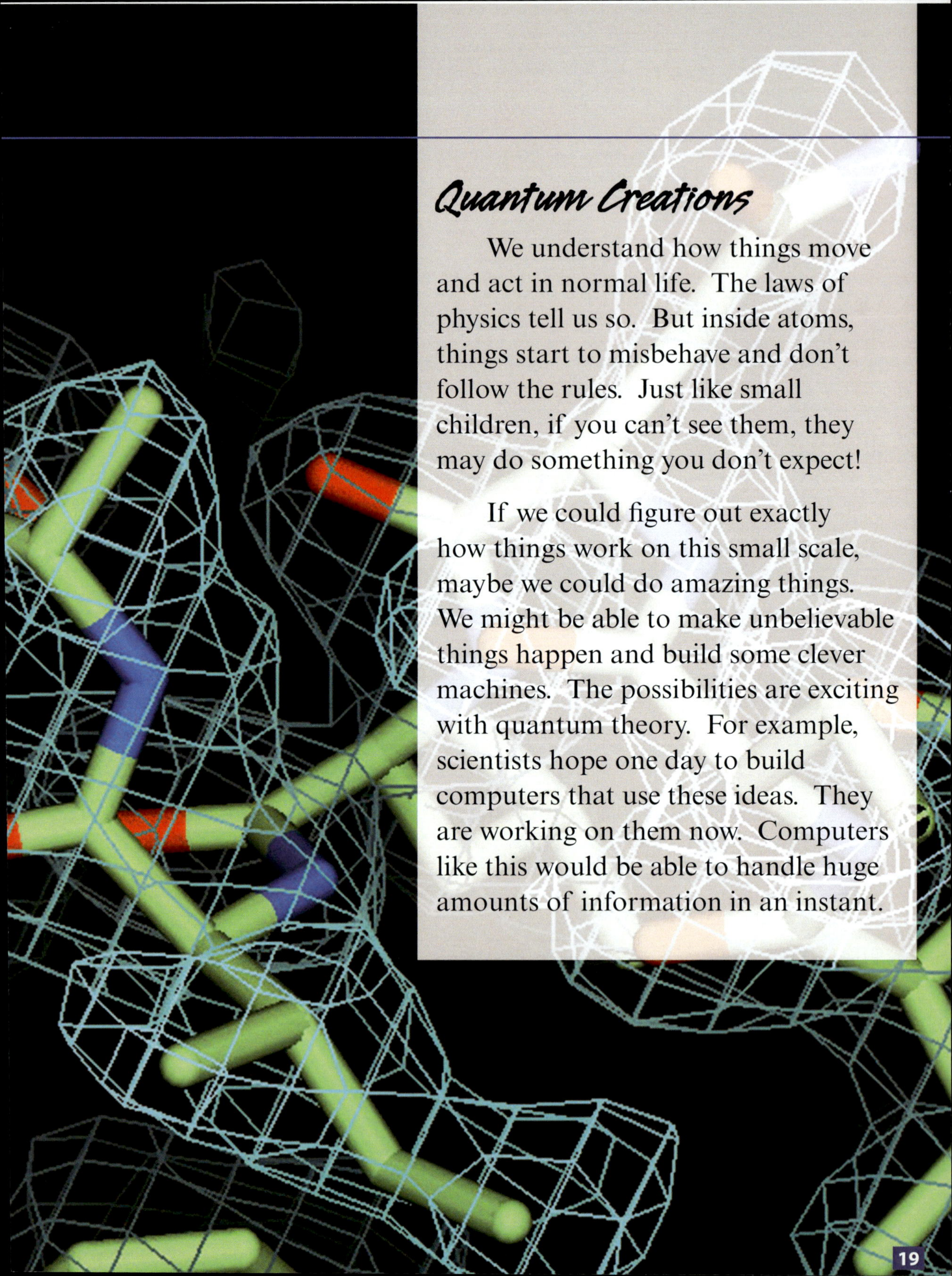

Quantum Creations

We understand how things move and act in normal life. The laws of physics tell us so. But inside atoms, things start to misbehave and don't follow the rules. Just like small children, if you can't see them, they may do something you don't expect!

If we could figure out exactly how things work on this small scale, maybe we could do amazing things. We might be able to make unbelievable things happen and build some clever machines. The possibilities are exciting with quantum theory. For example, scientists hope one day to build computers that use these ideas. They are working on them now. Computers like this would be able to handle huge amounts of information in an instant.

What Is a Laser?

Lasers were invented because of quantum theory. Lasers can be used for many things. For example, they can make holograms or perform surgery. They can print and read information on CDs and DVDs. It was over 40 years between the discovery of quantum theory and the invention of lasers. It makes you wonder what other things are waiting to be invented!

What is a laser? Normal light from the sun or a lamp is made of different colors. It comes out in all directions. The light from a laser is all the same color and is lined up in the same direction. Laser light is made by forcing electrons inside atoms to give out a set number of quanta. This is always the same for the atoms in a particular substance. That is why the light from one type of laser is always the same color.

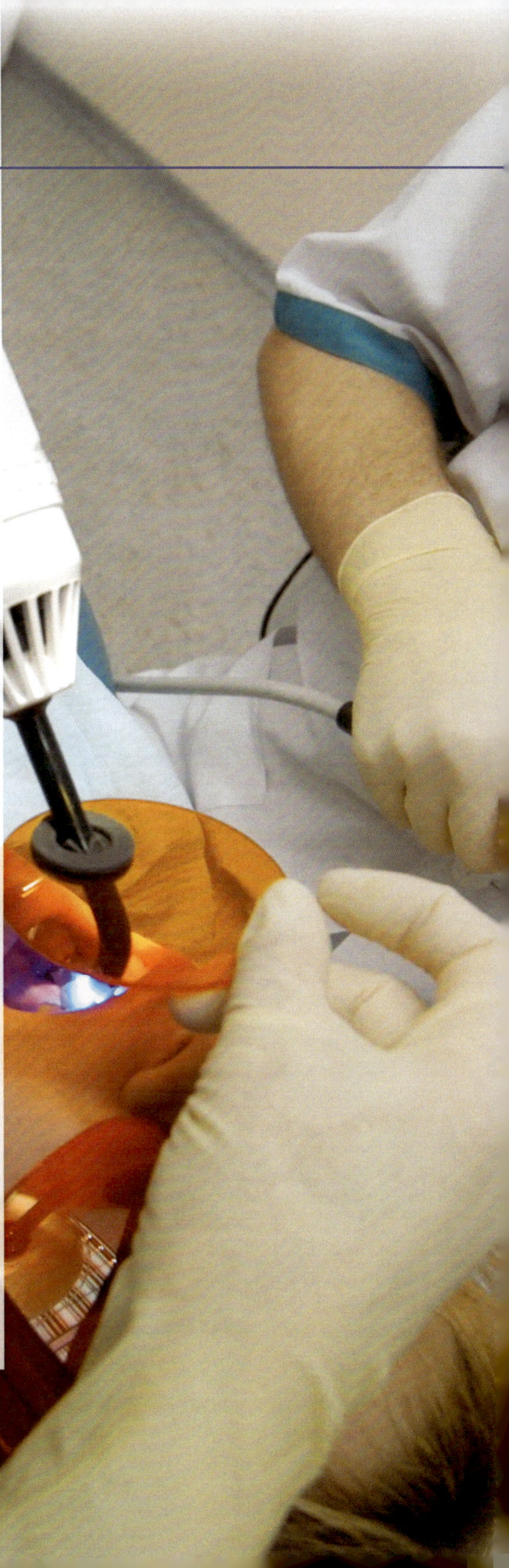

Speed of Light

In 1887, two scientists showed that light waves travel at the same speed everywhere all the time. This didn't make sense to people. They expected light to travel faster if the source was moving toward them. They thought it should be just like two cars coming at each other. From the point of view of the people in one car, the other car would be coming at them very fast! However, this doesn't work with light. That puzzled people.

Later, scientists were able to understand why this happens. They used Planck's quantum theory to figure it out. Who knows how much more quantum theory will help us to understand in the future?

No matter how fast the cars go, the light from their headlights still goes at the same speed.

Private Life

While doing his own studies, Planck taught others, too. He was a professor at his hometown college. After one of his own great teachers died, Planck took over the professor's job in Berlin.

Planck had a rich home life, too. It was also a sad one. In 1887, he married Marie Merck. They had two sons and twin daughters. Their home became a gathering place for other great scientists and thinkers. People came there to talk. They played music, too.

Planck and fellow scientist Albert Einstein

Planck and fellow scientist Niels Bohr

Planck

Some people think there is a strong link between people who like science and math and who also like to play music. This proved true among Planck and his friends.

The family was happy together for many years, but in 1909, Marie died. In 1911, Planck married his cousin, Marga von Hoesslin. They had one son together. Shortly after, Planck's oldest son was killed while fighting in World War I. A few years later, each of Planck's daughters died while giving birth to their children. The babies lived.

The years of the war were hard ones. It was a challenge to continue to work. Planck tried to support other scientists. He came up with the slogan, "Persevere and continue working." He wanted them to carry on their work. He knew it was important in making the world a better place.

Soldiers and Red Cross aides in one of the many trenches that were common during WWI

Sally Ride

Sally Ride grew up in Los Angeles, California. As a young girl, she loved science. Ride's parents encouraged her interest. She grew up playing with a chemistry set and a simple telescope. She also played sports and competed in national junior tennis tournaments.

Ride went to college and studied physics. She also played on the tennis team. One day, sh saw an ad in the school newspaper announcing that NASA was accepting applications for astronauts and, for the first time, was accepting women into the astronaut program. Of the 8,0 people who applied, Ride was one of 35 (including five other women) wh were accepted.

In 1983, Sally Ride became the first American woman to fly in space. During her historic flight aboard the space shuttle *Challenger*, she deployed communication satellites, operated the robot arm, and conducte experiments in Earth remote sensing. Ride made her second trip into spac one year later.

After leaving NASA, Ride became a professor of physics at the University of California, San Diego. In 2001, she started her own company, Sally Ride Science, to pursue her longtime passion: motivating young people, especially girls, to pursue their interests in science.

Sally Ride is best known as America's first woman in space. But among her most important work may be the inspiration to young people follow their dreams—just as she followed hers.

Isaac Newton and the Laws of the Universe

Jane Weir, MPhys

Physical Science Readers:
Isaac Newton and the Laws of the Universe

Publishing Credits

Editorial Director
Dona Herweck Rice

Associate Editor
Joshua BishopRoby

Editor-in-Chief
Sharon Coan, M.S.Ed.

Creative Director
Lee Aucoin

Illustration Manager
Timothy J. Bradley

Publisher
Rachelle Cracchiolo, M.S.Ed.

Science Contributor
Sally Ride Science

Science Consultants
Michael E. Kopecky,
Science Department Chair,
Chino Hills High School
Jane Weir, MPhys

Teacher Created Materials
5301 Oceanus Drive
Huntington Beach, CA 92649-1030
http://www.tcmpub.com

ISBN 978-0-7439-0574-9

Printed in China Wai002

Table of Contents

Let Newton Be!

Imagine a world where nobody knows why the Earth goes round the sun. Imagine that they don't know why things fall downward when dropped. Imagine a world without cars, television, or computers. That was the world before Isaac Newton.

Isaac Newton

Newton was born and grew up in the countryside.

On January 4, 1643, Isaac Newton was born in Lincolnshire, England. He arrived much too early and was very small. No one thought he would live. But he did. His mother said he was so small he could fit inside a quart mug.

Newton's father was a farmer. He died a few months before his son was born. When Newton was two years old, his mother remarried. She went to live with her new husband. She did not take her young son with her. Newton's stepfather would not let her take him. She left her son in the care of his grandmother. She and her new husband had three more children.

Newton was without his mother until the age of ten. At that time, his stepfather died. His mother and her children came home to be with Newton.

Birthday

Newton's birthday is January 4, 1643, if using the calendar we use today. But in Newton's time, a different calendar was used. According to that calendar, he was born on December 25, 1642, which is Christmas Day.

Newton went to the neighborhood school. At first he didn't do well. The teachers said he didn't pay attention. He was then sent to a bigger and better grammar school. It was called The King's School. He carved his name on the windowsill in the school library. People can still see it there today.

He became the best student at King's. They called this honor "top boy." While at this school, he lived with a local family. He became engaged to their daughter. When Newton left there for college, he focused on his studies. He didn't pay much attention to the girl back home. She married someone else. Newton never married anyone. People say that he always had warm feelings for his first love.

Newton's boyhood school still stands.

Statue of Aristotle

Newton's mother wanted him to be a farmer. He tried to please her. He tried farming before he tried college. But he couldn't stop thinking about his studies. He wasn't happy as a farmer. The head of King's school convinced his mother to send him to college.

The students in college studied Aristotle (AIR-uh-stot-uhl). He was a Greek philosopher from long ago. Newton wanted to study newer and better ideas. He took it upon himself to learn about modern philosophers and scientists.

Master of the Mint

In his later life, Newton was in charge of the Royal Mint. His job was to replace the old hand-made coins with new ones made by machines. He was also in charge of finding people who made fake money.

Absent-Minded Mathematician

Newton was absent-minded. Legend has it that Newton, when holding parties, would wander off to get refreshments for his guests but start working out a math problem instead. He would forget to go back to dinner!

The legend of Newton being hit on the head with an apple is how many people remember him.

Nature and nature's laws lay hid in night:
God said, "Let Newton be!" and all was light.

Alexander Pope, the famous English writer, said this about Newton. He meant that Newton was able to explain mysteries of nature that nobody else could.

In order to help his studies, Newton invented a new math. It was called **calculus** (KAL-kyuh-luhs). But he didn't like to talk about himself or his work. He didn't tell anyone about his new math for 30 years.

Alexander Pope

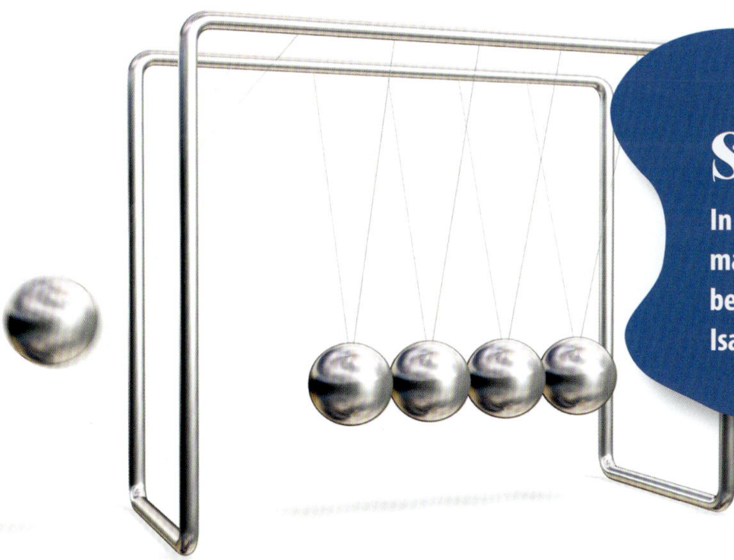

Sir Knight

In 1705, Newton was made a royal knight. He became known as Sir Isaac Newton.

This toy is called a Newton's Cradle. It illustrates some of Newton's discoveries about motion.

Newton was very good at using math to describe things that he saw happen in nature. Motion is one of these things. Motion is caused by **force**. Newton did not know what caused the forces of nature. But he knew he could measure their effects, such as motion. This is what he spent most of his life working on.

The measurement of forces are required to send a rocket into space.

Laura Bassi (1711-1778)

Laura Bassi was one of the first women ever to earn a doctorate (DOK-ter-it) degree. That is the highest degree a person can earn. She was also one of the first to become a paid professor at a university. In school, she studied all types of science and math. She also learned four languages. Bassi married a fellow teacher. They had 12 children. She continued to work while she raised her children. She fought to be given greater responsibility at the university. She also fought for better pay and better equipment to do experiments in physics. She was one of the first scientists to study and follow the teachings of Newton.

Newton's Ideas

Principia

Newton wrote a famous book about forces and the way things move. This book has a long name in Latin. It is called the *Principia* for short. It is one of the most important scientific books ever written.

Newton didn't like showing off his work. He only published his book because his friends urged him. One friend even paid for it to be published.

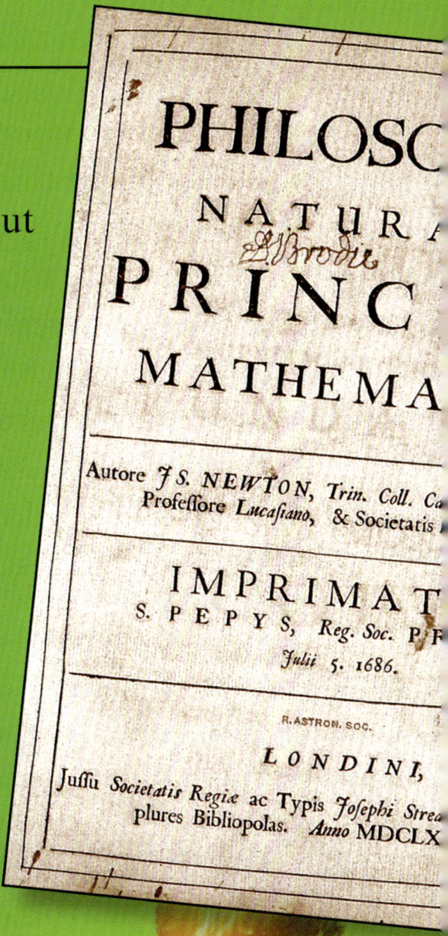

PHILOSO
NATURA
PRINC
MATHEMA

Autore *J S.* NEWTON, *Trin. Coll.* Ca
Professore *Lucasiano*, & Societatis

IMPRIMAT
S. PEPYS, *Reg. Soc.* P
Julii 5. 1686.

R.ASTRON. SOC.

LONDINI,
Jussu *Societatis Regiæ* ac Typis *Josephi* Strea
plures Bibliopolas. *Anno* MDCLX

Newton's *Principia*, published in 1687

The book has three parts. The first part is about gravity. Newton shows that gravity makes everything that has **mass** attract everything else. The second part is about how things move in substances such as air and water. The third part is about the motion of planets and other bodies in space.

Newtonian Mechanics

Newton described forces so well that the math used now to figure how things move is named after him. It is called Newtonian Mechanics. Using this math, we can map the path of a strawberry as it falls through the air into a bowl. We can work out how fast a stone will fall after it is dropped. We can figure out how much effort is needed to pick up a book. We can explain the moon's path around Earth. In fact, the movement of anything we see can be explained with Newton's system.

The strawberries falling portray gravity, which was explained in Newton's first law. The strawberries displacing the milk portray Newton's second law.

A Dark Force?

Philosophers in Newton's time criticized his theory of gravity because he didn't explain what caused it. They thought it made gravity sound like a mysterious, dark force. That frightened them. Newton refused to guess at what gravity actually is. He just stuck to describing the way it moves things.

The Newton

The standard international (SI) unit used to measure force is the **newton**, named after Isaac Newton.

Laws of Motion

Newton is perhaps most famous for three laws about the way things move. Newton didn't write the laws. Other scientists studying his work wrote them. They called them Newton's Laws of Motion. Newtonian Mechanics is based on the Laws of Motion.

Newton's First Law

Newton's First Law of Motion is the law of **inertia** (in-UR-shuh). Inertia means resistance to changes in motion. The law says that an object will keep doing what it's doing so long as an unbalanced force doesn't act on it. This works for things that are still and for things that are moving. Things that are still will stay still. Things that are moving will keep moving in a straight line with the same speed.

According to Newton's First Law, a bicycle won't change its motion until something makes it change.

Newton's Second Law

Newton's Second Law is the law of **acceleration**. It describes what happens when you apply a force to an object. It says that the bigger the force, the more the object speeds up or slows down. It also says that the object will always move in the same direction of the force. A bigger force is needed to make a heavier object speed up or slow down by the same amount as a light object. This makes sense. For example, a bowling ball is harder to throw than a tennis ball. It is harder to stop a car than a bicycle.

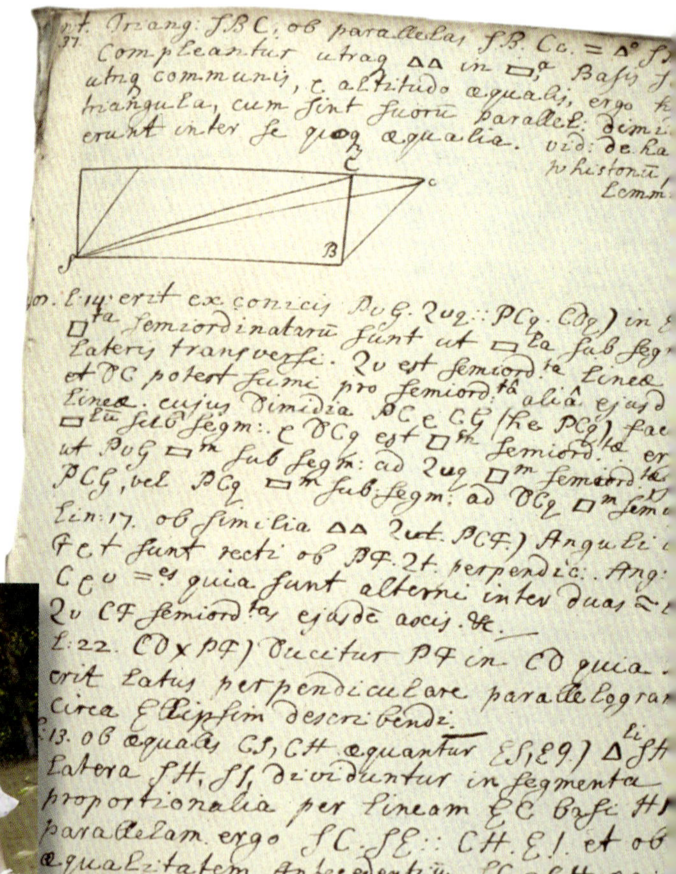

This is an actual page out of Isaac Newton's manuscript.

It takes a bigger force to push an adult on a swing than it takes to push a child.

Newton's Third Law

Newton's Third Law of Motion is the law of action and reaction. For every action, there is an equal and opposite reaction. So whenever a force pushes on an object, the object pushes back in the opposite direction. The force of the object pushing back is called the reaction force.

This law explains many things. For example, it explains why we can move a rowboat in water with an oar. The water pushes back on the oar as much as the oar pushes on the water. This moves the boat. It also explains why a chair stays where it is instead of crashing through the floor. The floor pushes back and keeps it there. Also, when you hit a baseball with a bat, the ball pushes on the bat as much as the bat pushes on the ball. Hit it just right, and all that force creates a home run!

Fun in Motion

They may or may not know it, but snowboarders use forces and motion to perform stunts. As a snowboarder travels downhill, she picks up speed because she is being accelerated by gravity. The reaction force of the slope pushes her away from the slope and forward. Friction and air resistance both oppose her motion and act to slow her down. She can use wax on the base of her board to reduce friction between the board and snow and to make her go faster. She can tuck down to reduce drag, which speeds her up, too. When she tips the board to one side, she changes the direction the reaction force is acting in. This makes her turn. As she pulls an ollie (a type of jump on the board), she can bend, twist, and lean to change the center of gravity of her body on the board and keep herself steady.

The force of the ball on the bat as it is hit is called the reaction force. It is created in reaction to the force made by the swinging bat.

Imagine trying to throw a snowball without gravity. If you threw the snowball in the air, then it would just disappear into space and never come back!

Gravity

Newton realized that the force that makes planets go around the sun is the same force that makes things fall to Earth. It is called **gravity** (GRAV-i-tee). A story about Newton says that he figured out gravity when he saw an apple fall from a tree. He realized that the apple and the moon are similar. Gravity attracts them both to Earth.

Gravity is what holds us on the ground. It keeps us from floating into space. It also keeps Earth going around the sun. And it keeps the moon going around Earth. Without gravity, things would just bob in space.

Newton watched the planets in the sky. He figured out that the planets were pulled towards the sun. The closer the planets were to the sun, the stronger the pull on them.

:scape!

ʻ you can make something go fast nough, it will have enough energy ɔ escape Earth's gravity and go into rbit. Earth's escape velocity is 11 ilometers (7 miles) per second, ʻhich is very fast. This is how space ehicles are able to leave Earth.

Emilie de Breteuil (1706-1749)

De Breteuil was born into a wealthy family in France. Her family thought her job was to marry well, but her father thought she was too tall for anyone to marry her. (She was 5 feet and 9 inches tall.) He gave her a very good education to make up for it. She did marry at 19, but she had already learned a great deal. After her third child was born, she began to study the work of Newton. She translated his *Principia* into French. Her translation is still used today. It became the reason why Newton's work was well known in France. She also wrote a textbook on physics for her child. And she built a private lab at her estate. When she became pregnant again at the age of 42, she was afraid she wouldn't live through the birth. She worked so hard she barely slept. She wanted to be sure to finish all the work she could. She died six days after the birth, but she had finished her work.

He also watched the moon. He learned that the moon was pulled towards the Earth. If Earth's gravity stopped pulling on it, the moon would head off in a straight line away from Earth. This is Newton's first law. Earth's gravity gives it a constant tug. This pulls it around in a circle. Think of a ball on a string. If you swing the ball around your head, then the tension in the string acts like gravity. It keeps the ball moving in a circle. The ball would fly off at an angle if you were to let go of the string. This is what would happen to the moon if Earth's gravity stopped working.

The moon has energy from its motion. That is why Earth's gravity doesn't make the moon fall down and land on Earth. If something came along that stopped the moon from moving, then it would start falling toward Earth. Just as in the ball example, if you let the ball slow down too much, then it will collapse toward you!

Gravity keeps the moon from pulling away from Earth, just as this string keeps the ball in motion from being thrown away from the post.

Why Does a Roller Coaster Make Your Tummy Go Funny?

When you jump off something high or go down a steep slope on a roller coaster, you are under the influence of gravity. You feel weightless when this happens because there is no reaction force pressing up under you. In a roller coaster, gravity is acting on your seat and accelerating (ak-SEL-uh-rate-ing) it downward at the same rate as you. That's why it doesn't push upward with a reaction force like a seat usually does. Your insides can move about, but the inside of your body is made mostly of water, so there is more **drag** there than outside. This stops some of your internal organs from being accelerated as fast as the outside of your body at first. So, you feel a jolt (like your stomach coming up into your mouth) until the outside of your body catches up with your insides and forces them to accelerate with the rest of your body!

Light

Newton disagreed with the theories of his time about light. People thought that **white light** was natural light. They thought that colored light was made when light went through air or water and was changed. They thought that a rainbow (called a **spectrum**) comes from a **prism** (PRIZ-uhm) because the prism changes the light.

Newton did an experiment with two glass prisms. He showed that, if the spectrum coming from one prism was put through another prism, the colors didn't change again. So he knew that white light must be made of all the colors of the rainbow. It was just broken up into different colors through the prism. From this, people could explain why rainbows happen.

Newton changed people's understanding of light. But many people criticized his ideas. He got tired of defending them. So he didn't publish his work on light until 30 years after he completed it.

White light is composed of all the colors in the rainbow at once. A prism separates the different colors in white light so you can see them individually.

Humble Scientist

Newton was modest about his achievements. He once said that, if he had seen further than other people, it was because he had stood on the shoulders of giants. This meant that he recognized that his discoveries had their roots in the ideas of scientists who had gone before him.

Inventions

Newton invented many gadgets. Some of them are still used today. He invented a **reflecting microscope** (MY-kruh-skope). He designed and built the first **reflector telescope** (TEL-uh-skope). They both use mirrors. Before this, all telescopes used lenses. Lenses are curved pieces of glass such as those used in eyeglasses. The type of telescope that Newton invented is still used. It is very good for looking at groups of stars. It is called the Newtonian telescope.

Quality lenses were important to Newton. He decided to play with lenses and a glass plate to see what he could figure out. He showed that shining a light on the lens and plate at a certain angle could produce rings of light. We call these **Newton's Rings**. They are used for testing the quality of lens surfaces.

Sextants used a viewfinder tube to find stars in the sky and a metal rim with measurements on it to find latitude.

Newton's Rings

Newton also wrote a formula to describe how far away a lens will focus light. This is called the lens equation. It is useful for making anything with a lens in it. In fact, Newton ground his own lenses for his telescopes.

Sailors of his time owed thanks to Newton. He designed the **sextant**. The sextant helped sailors to find their position at sea. They used the sun and stars to do it.

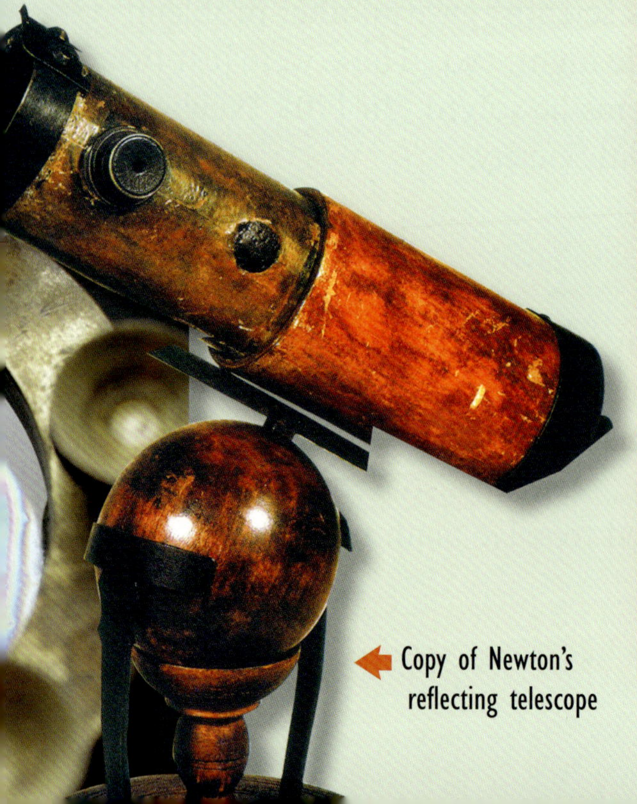

Copy of Newton's reflecting telescope

Newton's Chicken

Newton is such a famous and important scientist that everyone knows about him. He's so well-known that people even tell jokes about him. Here are some answers to a famous joke that tell about Newton's laws of motion and gravity.

Why did the chicken cross the road?

First Law of Motion: Chickens at rest stay at rest. Chickens in motion cross the road.

Second Law of Motion: The chicken was pushed.

Third Law of Motion: The chicken was pushed by another chicken who knocked itself over by pushing so hard.

Law of Gravity: The chicken was attracted to a bigger chicken waiting across the road.

Secret Solver

In 1662, the Royal Society was set up in England. This was like a "clever scientists club." It supported research and discovery in science. Scientists met and talked about things that puzzled them. Sometimes they gave a problem to one another as a challenge. Newton was very good at solving their problems.

In 1696, a Swiss **mathematician** (math-uh-muh-TISH-uhn) gave a problem for all the math experts of Europe to solve. He gave them six months to do it. Newton solved it in a single night. He didn't like discussing his math proofs, so he published the answer anonymously in a Royal Society magazine. (In fact, Newton didn't publish any of his math texts under his own name until he was 60 years old.)

When another famous scientist gave another problem, Newton solved it in a single night, too. These were just two of many difficult math problems he solved. In 1703, Newton was made president of the Royal Society.

A New Branch of Math

Newton invented a way of using math to go back and forth between things that are related, like surface area and volume, or speed and acceleration. His method is now called calculus. It is a whole branch of math. Newton also wrote a rule called the **binomial theorem**. It is used to solve math problems.

Royal Society Hall

Albert Einstein

Gentle Genius

Don Herweck

Physical Science Readers:
Albert Einstein: Gentle Genius

Publishing Credits

Editorial Director
Dona Herweck Rice

Associate Editor
Joshua BishopRoby

Editor-in-Chief
Sharon Coan, M.S.Ed.

Creative Director
Lee Aucoin

Illustration Manager
Timothy J. Bradley

Publisher
Rachelle Cracchiolo, M.S.Ed.

Science Contributor
Sally Ride Science

Science Consultants
Michael E. Kopecky,
Science Department Chair,
Chino Hills High School
Jane Weir, MPhys

Teacher Created Materials
5301 Oceanus Drive
Huntington Beach, CA 92649-1030
http://www.tcmpub.com

ISBN 978-0-7439-0572-5

Table of Contents

Early Life

Albert Einstein may be the most famous **physicist** of all time. He is known both for his brilliant mind and his gentle spirit. He thought of things no one ever had. But he always stayed humble. He believed he was just one small part of the world, trying to figure things out.

Einstein was born in March of 1879 in Ulm, Germany. His family owned a business there. They made parts for machines. These parts helped the machines run on electricity.

Einstein didn't talk much when he was little. Some people thought he was not smart. He later proved this was far from true.

When Einstein was five years old and sick in bed, his father showed him a compass from the shop. Einstein realized that something made the needle move. That "something" was **magnetism**. He later said that moment was very important to him. It made him want to study science. He built models and mechanical things for fun.

Einstein, shown here with his sister Maja in about 1884, enjoyed physics-related puzzles even when he was a young boy.

He taught himself geometry by the age of 12. He was bored with regular school and often got into trouble there. He found ways to learn on his own. The family shop was a big help to his learning.

A compass

Einstein as a boy

Amazing Brain

After he died, Einstein's brain was studied. They found that it had an unusual shape. Some scientists think that the shape of his brain may have made him both slow when young and very smart at the same time.

Einstein's family moved often during his life. When he was one, they moved to Munich, Germany. Then, the family moved to Milan, Italy. Einstein was 15 at the time. He stayed behind in Germany for school. He wrote his first scientific work during this time away from his family. It was a paper on magnetism.

Einstein disliked his school very much. He loved to learn, but he didn't love his school's way of teaching. He finally left the school. He followed his family to Italy.

Einstein in the Bern patent office

Einstein's family wanted him to graduate. In 1896, they sent him to Switzerland to finish school. He trained to be a teacher of physics and math. When he couldn't find a teaching job, he took a job at the Swiss patent office. He became an assistant technical examiner. This meant that he had to review applications from inventors.

This clock tower in Bern existed in Einstein's time and still works today.

Important Scientist

Isaac Newton (1643–1727) was an English scientist, mathematician, and inventor. His three laws of motion are very important in physics. His work was key to the work that Einstein would later do.

Marriage and Family

Einstein married Mileva Maric in 1903. They had one daughter and two sons. Their marriage ended in 1919. In that year, he married his cousin, Elsa Löwenthal. She died in 1936.

Portrait of Albert Einstein, 1947, about the same time that he began writing his most prominent theories

Einstein's specialty at the office was electromagnetic devices. He knew quite a bit about such things. He had learned a lot in his family's shop. This made his job easy. It gave him time to think about physics and the things he found important.

On his own time, he began to write science papers filled with new ideas. Once his ideas got out, the world would never be the same.

Einstein sent one of his papers to a university. They awarded him a doctoral degree. He sent another paper to another university. They made him a speaker at the school. He was made a professor of physics at a third university. By the age of 30, he was considered by many to be one of the world's leading scientific thinkers.

Einstein is known for solving a number of tough problems. Scientists of his time could not find the answers to these problems. They were using old ideas. They thought about things in old ways. Einstein found new ways to look at the problems. His new ideas changed the world.

Happy As Is

Einstein was known for being a bit of a slob. He didn't think formal dress was all that important. And he didn't like to wear socks. He said, "When I was young, I found out that the big toe always ends up making a hole in the sock. So, I stopped wearing socks."

Work That Changed the World

The year 1905 was a great one for Einstein. It was great for th
world of science, too. He wrote four important papers. They beca
the building blocks for modern physics. It was also the year he ear
his advanced degree.

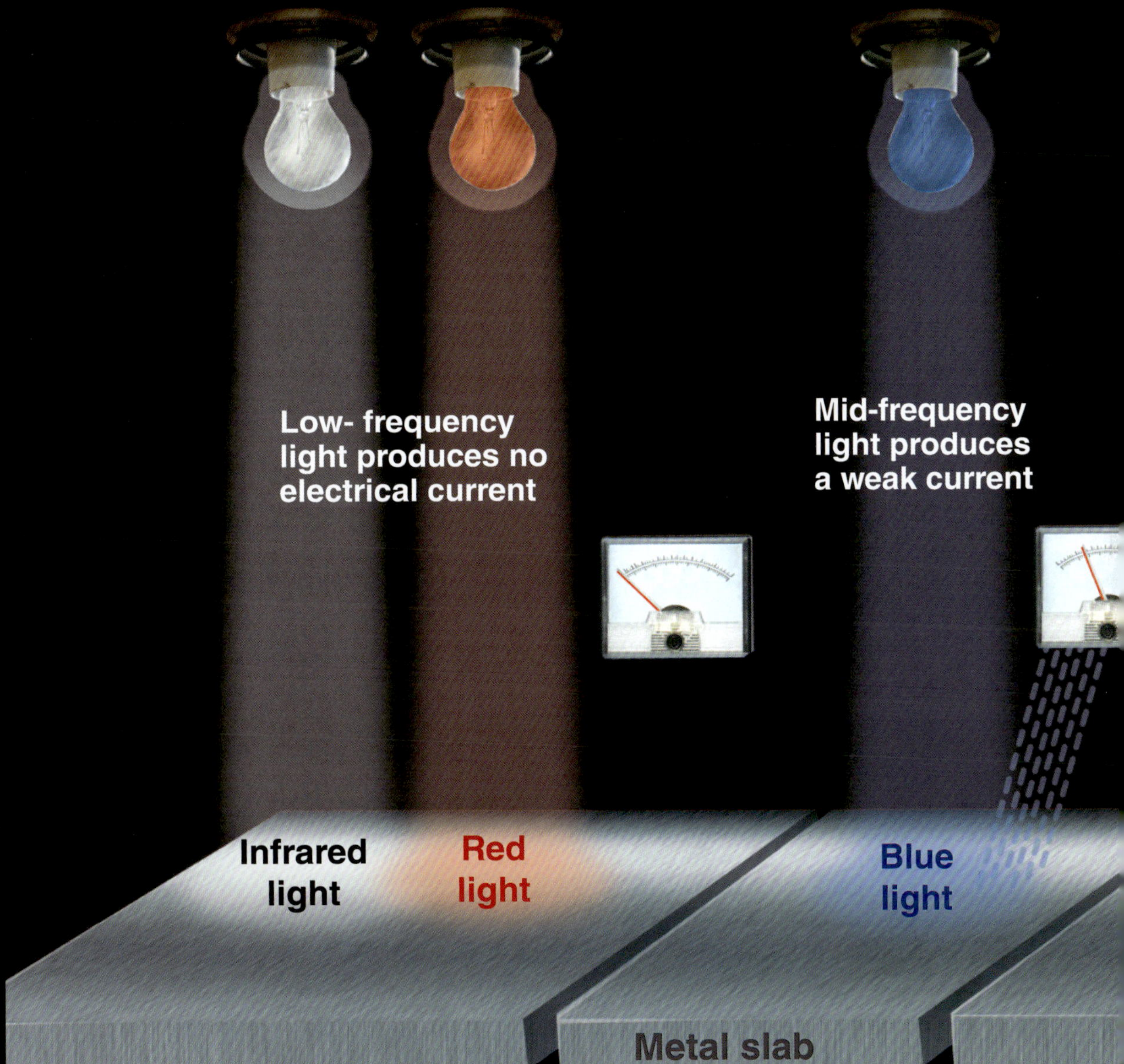

Photoelectric Effect and Light Quanta

Einstein's first paper explained the **photoelectric effect**. Scientists had noticed something strange. They shined a bright light onto a metal surface. An electric current would run through the metal. They didn't know why this happened.

The paper started by explaining the work of other scientists. Einstein used math to describe the reasons for what they found. He explained why a small current flows through metal when light shines on it. He also explained that the current depends on color, and he told why this is.

Einstein experimented with colored light. He showed that blue light makes a current, while red does not. He also found that **ultraviolet light** makes a larger current than the blue light does.

What did it mean? Einstein wasn't finished.

Later, fellow scientist Max Planck would use Einstein's work on the photoelectric effect in his own work, for which he won the Nobel Prize. Planck managed to figure out the basic value of energy that one particle of light contains.

Einstein pointed out that different lights created different amounts of electrical **energy**. The amount of energy depended on the **light wave**.

Scientists knew that light traveled in waves. Red light has very low **frequency** waves. Blue light has higher frequency waves. Ultraviolet frequency is very high. The higher the frequency, the more energy the light wave has.

Einstein showed that the more energy is in the light wave, the more electricity it produces in the metal on which it shines. The light's energy was turned into electricity.

Einstein Said

"The most incomprehensible thing about the universe is t it's comprehensible." Einstei meant it is amazing to know that the world's mysteries ca be figured out.

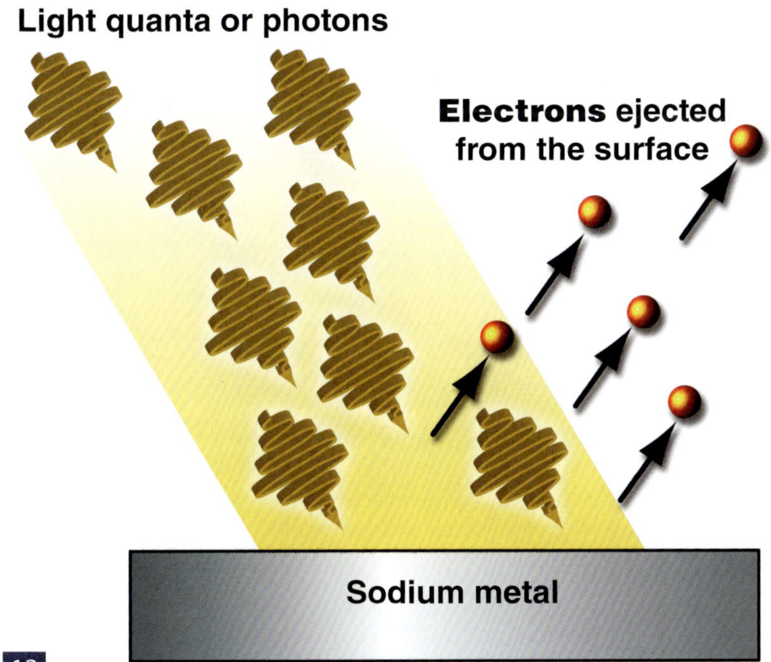

Einstein's paper described **quanta**, or individual packets of energy. Light waves push these quanta around. Today, we call them photons. He explained that quanta cause the photoelectric effect.

Einstein won the Nob Prize in physics in 1921 fo this work with light quant

Why Is the Sky Blue?

One example of light and color is right above us. It is in the sky and its blue color. Why is the sky blue? The answer is explained with light waves. Light waves are absorbed and scattered at different rates. Light with short wavelengths (such as blue) is scattered more than light with longer wavelengths (such as red). In the case of light from the sun, the blue waves are absorbed easily by dust, water, and other particles as light travels from the sun to Earth. As the blue light waves are absorbed, they are also scattered in different directions. So when you look into the sky, what you are really seeing are blue light waves scattered everywhere.

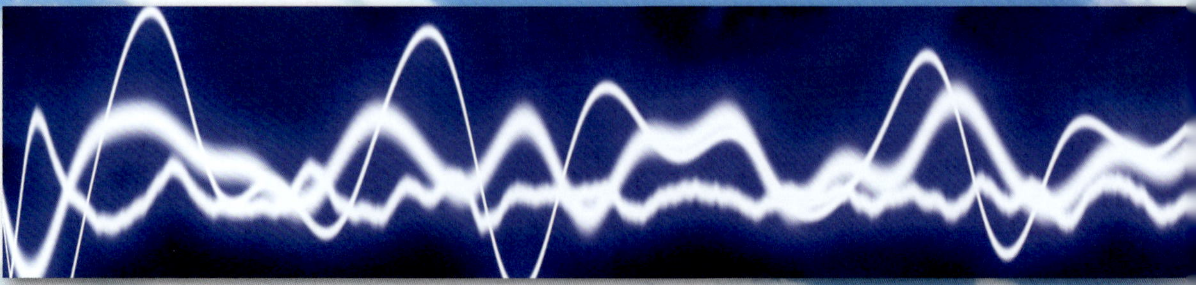

Brownian Motion

Einstein's second paper explained **Brownian motion**. In 1827, Robert Brown was studying pollen grains. He looked at them in water through a microscope. He noticed that the pollen grains moved around in the water. He didn't know why this happened.

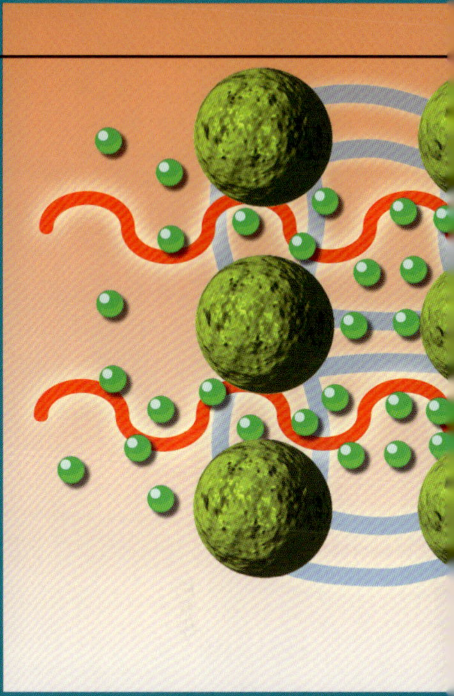

Einstein explained this movement. The water drop was made of billions of water molecules. The reason the pollen grains move is due to the **molecules** (MOL-uh-kules) of the water hitting them. The pollen grain moves in random directions because the molecules hit from all different sides.

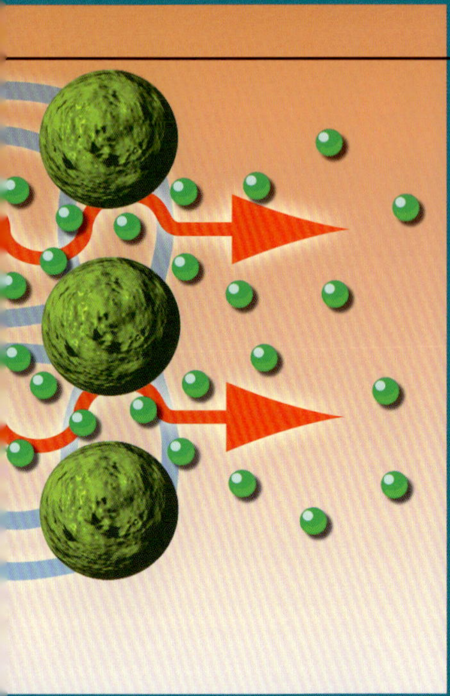

In this diagram of Brownian motion, the large green pollen grains are jostled about by the much smaller water molecules, which are always moving around.

In the Brownian assembly, the beach balls are jostled about by the students.

Brownian "Assembly"

To better understand random Brownian motion, think of a school assembly. Imagine everyone there. What would happen if all these people moved into a classroom? They would be tightly packed with little or no room. Now, imagine putting some huge beach balls in the room. They would stay in place because nothing in the room is in motion. So, what happens if everyone tried to move? The balls will be forced to move, although not very much. If everyone tries to run around the room, some of the people will be forced out the door. The balls will move faster and farther. The distance between people will increase. The temperature will even rise in the room. This is what happens with Brownian motion.

Special Theory of Relativity

The third paper of 1905 describes Einstein's **special theory of relativity** (rel-uh-TIV-uh-tee). It solved a problem with how people understood light.

At the time, scientists believed that light waves worked like waves in the ocean. Ocean waves travel through the water. They thought light waves had to travel through something, too. They called this substance *ether*. There was one problem. Two scientists made an experiment to measure the ether. They couldn't find any.

Einstein's paper started with the work of other scientists. He used their math to explain that light did not need to travel through anything. Light was different from ocean waves. Light always traveled at the same speed. That speed was a very big number. Instead of always writing the number, Einstein just wrote *c*.

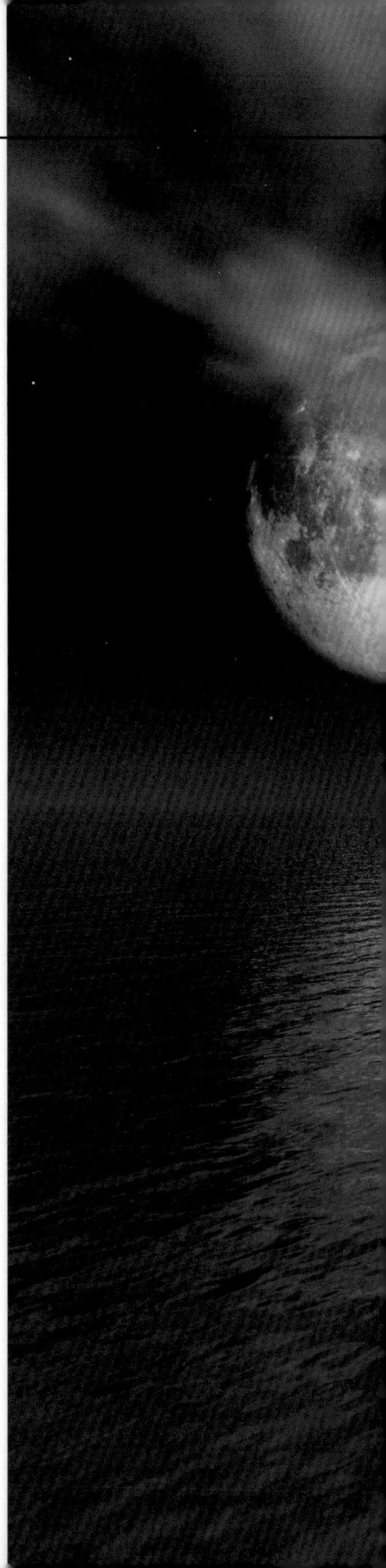

Albert Michelson

Edward Morley

About Ether

Albert Michelson and Edward Morley weren't trying to disprove ether, but that's what they did. They made an experiment to measure how fast the ether carried light. They thought ether was moving. If they shined a light in the direction ether was going, the light should go faster. If they shined a light the other way, it would slow down. No matter which direction they shined the light, though, the speed was always the same. Ether wasn't carrying the light. It didn't exist.

Super Genius, Poor Speller

Einstein spoke and read both German and English fluently. But he was a terrible speller. He said he wasn't able to write English because he spelled so poorly.

Einstein wasn't done, though. Light was *very* different from ocean waves.

If you were on a sailing ship, you could travel along with the waves. From where you stood on the deck, the waves might look like they did not move. You could even travel faster than the waves. Then, the waves would look like they were going backwards!

Light works differently. Light always looks like it travels at *c*. Imagine you have a fast bicycle and your friend has a flashlight. Your friend shines the flashlight and you pedal in the same direction. No matter how fast you go, the light will still shine ahead as if you were standing still. How could that be? Einstein had the answer.

Einstein said that the faster you go, the slower time goes. At the same time, everything gets shorter. The front of your bike will shrink back toward the end of your bike. The more you try to catch the light, the slower time goes and the shorter you get. We don't notice this in everyday life. This only happens close to the speed of light.

Einstein showed that the old definitions of space and time had to be changed. They were two parts of the same thing, called *spacetime*. The faster you went, the weirder things got.

The girl is watching the bike rider travel near the speed of light. Notice that the bike rider's shape appears shortened.

While traveling near the speed of light, the world appears blurry to the bike rider.

Karen Magnus

Dr. Magnus is an American Indian. She is also a skilled scientist. She uses the high energy of X-rays to figure out the structure of a substance's atoms. She does this with crystals. When an X-ray hits a crystal, the X-ray diffracts. That means it breaks apart. This is like what happens when sunlight breaks apart to become a rainbow. The way that it diffracts tells about the structure of the atoms. Magnus says, "My scientific work has taught me . . . about flexibility, and the fact that you always have to be able to change your mind. For example, you may come up with a hypothesis, but your experiments may not show the results you expected. When this happens you have to be able to admit you were incorrect and move on!"

$E = mc^2$

Einstein's fourth paper in 1905 tells about the relationship between energy and **mass**. It says that the energy of a body (E) equals its mass (m) times the speed of light (c) squared. This is written $E = mc^2$.

The equation shows that mass and energy are linked. It means that energy must behave the same as mass does. Not only were space and time the same thing. Mass and energy were the same thing, too!

This can be observed during a solar eclipse. A solar eclipse occurs when the moon comes between the sun and Earth, blocking the sun's bright light. During this time, we can see that starlight bends when it passes the sun. Light is energy that falls toward the sun, just as mass does.

A solar eclipse in three stages

Louis Pasteur and the Fight Against Germs

Lisa Zamosky

Life Science Readers: Louis Pasteur and the Fight Against Germs

Publishing Credits

Editorial Director
Dona Herweck Rice

Associate Editor
Joshua BishopRoby

Editor-in-Chief
Sharon Coan, M.S.Ed.

Creative Director
Lee Aucoin

Illustration Manager
Timothy J. Bradley

Publisher
Rachelle Cracchiolo, M.S.Ed.

Science Contributor
Sally Ride Science™

Science Consultants
Thomas R. Ciccone, B.S., M.A.Ed.,
Chino Hills High School
Dr. Ronald Edwards,
DePaul University

Teacher Created Materials
5301 Oceanus Drive
Huntington Beach, CA 92649-1030
http://www.tcmpub.com

ISBN 978-0-7439-0588-6

Printed in China
Nordica.012019.CA21801586

Table of Contents

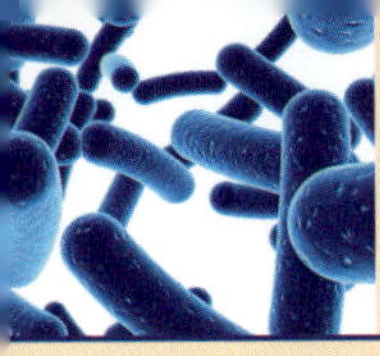

The Great French Scientist

Louis Pasteur

Notebooks Tell All

Pasteur kept many notebooks. He wrote down notes about all his lab experiments. He described over 100 experiments. Many years later, the notebooks were shared with the public. Scientists found that Pasteur did not always do his experiments the way he said he had. Sometimes, he changed the outcome to make his work look better. But the notebooks also showed years of hard work.

Louis Pasteur (pas-TUR) was a great scientist. He was born in France in 1822. He has been called the founder of modern medicine.

Pasteur is famous for many things. He saved millions of lives through his discoveries. He proved that germs spread disease. A germ is a simple living thing. It can only be seen with a **microscope**. A germ is also called a **microbe**. Can you guess what the study of small living things is called? It is called **microbiology**.

Pasteur may be best known for one of his inventions. It is a process named after him. It is called **pasteurization** (PAS-chur-i-ZAY-shun). It can be done with such liquids as milk and wine. The liquids are heated. The heat kills **bacteria** and **molds**. Pasteur saved many industries in France. His invention saved the beer, wine, and silk businesses.

A scientist uses a computer to display the image of a fly's eye as seen through a powerful microscope.

Microscope Power

Have you ever looked through a microscope? A microscope makes things look bigger. There are different kinds of microscopes. Pocket ones can magnify up to 30 times. Optical microscopes can magnify things up to 2,000 times. Electron microscopes are the most powerful. They can magnify up to one million times!

Have you ever seen a fly's face up close? With a microscope, you can see a fly's mouth. You can even see its eyes. If you looked at it, you would be able to see that it actually has more than two eyes. Each of its eyes is made of many smaller lenses. They let a fly see nearly everywhere at once!

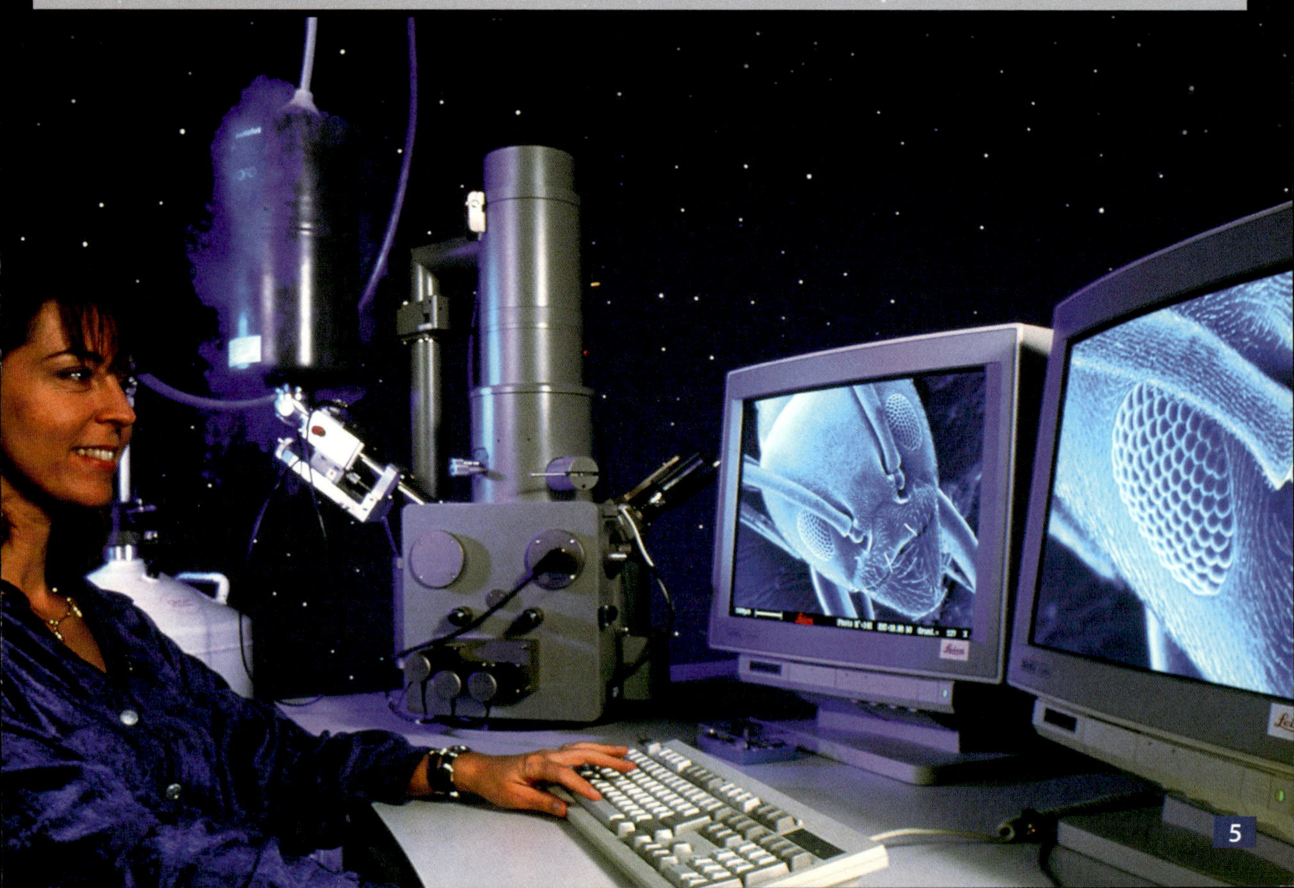

Early Years

Pasteur came from a family of **tanners**. Tanners are people who turn animal hides into leather. As a young boy, Pasteur was only an average student. He preferred to go fishing. His main interest was drawing. He drew many pictures of his family and friends.

Pasteur became a much better student as a teenager. He won many awards in school. His headmaster saw that he was very smart. He wanted Pasteur to apply to a college in Paris. It trained people to be **professors** in the sciences or arts. Very few people were accepted.

He went to Paris at the age of 15, but Pasteur was too homesick to stay. His father came to pick him up. He didn't even take the test to get in.

Pasteur was born in Dole, France. Paris was a long way from home.

tanners at work in the 1800s

A Lucky Star?

Pasteur made many discoveries during his lifetime. Some people said that he was lucky. He didn't agree. He said that you could only be lucky if your mind is prepared. He was successful because he paid attention. He noticed the small things in life.

So Serious

Young Pasteur drew pictures of many people. But they were never smiling. He was a serious person all through his life.

Entry into Chemistry

Pasteur didn't get to go to the school in Paris. So he attended a college near his home. He earned his science degree there. Soon after, he went back to the school in Paris. He took the entrance exam and passed it. The following year, he began studying **chemistry**. He worked hard, but he was never a great student.

Pasteur as a young man

Pasteur finished his doctor of science degree when he was only 26 years old. He had been studying the nature of **crystals**. He focused on certain crystals. He was interested in ones that formed in barrels of grapes. They were the ones used to make wine. Two acids had been discovered in France. Both were made of the same chemicals. Even so, they behaved very differently. Pasteur saw something special under his microscope. The surfaces of the two crystals were different. No one had noticed this before. He wrote and presented a paper about this.

Testing Himself

Pasteur took the Paris school's entrance exam twice. The first time, he received the 15th-highest score. This was good enough to be accepted. But it wasn't good enough for him. He wanted to do better. He did not enter school when he was accepted. Instead he took the test again. The second time, he received the fourth highest score. After that, he entered the school.

Sensational Science

Chemistry is the study of what things are made of and how they act under different conditions. It involves all the senses. It involves touch and smell. It involves sight and sound. It even involves taste.

Do you wonder why some people cry when they peel onions? How is makeup made? Why do some foods go bad so quickly? All these things can be answered by using simple chemistry.

crystals under a microscope

Professor Pasteur

After graduating, Pasteur worked as an assistant to one of his teachers. A couple of years later, he became a professor at a university. He taught chemistry. There, he continued to study crystals. He received many honors for his work.

Not long after becoming a professor, Pasteur met Marie Laurent (luh-RAWN). She was the daughter of a university official. Pasteur fell in love with her the moment he saw her. He wrote to her father. He asked for her hand in marriage. Her father gave his permission. The two were married for 46 years and had five children. Tragically, three of their daughters died of **typhoid fever** while they were young.

Late for an Important Date!

On the day before Pasteur's wedding, he went to his lab to work. He got so involved that his friend had to remind him to go to the church the next morning!

Louis and Marie Pasteur

Pasteur worked all the time, but it is said that he and his wife had a happy marriage. She knew how much he loved science. She understood his need to work hard. In the evenings, they worked together. He dictated his notes to her.

This is Strasbourg, France, where Pasteur taught and first met his wife.

Legion of Honor

The Legion of Honor medal is an award given to people who provide a great service to France. Pasteur won this award.

Afraid of Germs

Pasteur knew that germs spread easily. He never shook people's hands. He was afraid of germs. He would not even shake the hands of kings and queens.

Louis Pasteur in his laboratory

Focus on Fermentation

Pasteur moved to the University of Lille. There he became dean of sciences. He was only 32 years old. Lille was a city full of industry. Pasteur thought the science he taught should be useful. He wanted people to be able to use it in everyday life.

The father of one of Pasteur's students made alcohol. He was having problems with his product. So he came to Pasteur for help. He made alcohol from beet juice. He used **yeast** to change the sugar in the juice into alcohol. This process is called **fermentation**. The problem was that the alcohol he made was turning bad.

Fermentation became the focus of Pasteur's research. He studied the alcohol. Then he began studying milk. He found that there was yeast in both. Yeast is a very small life form that can grow in food. People used some yeasts in fermentation, but they did not know much about it.

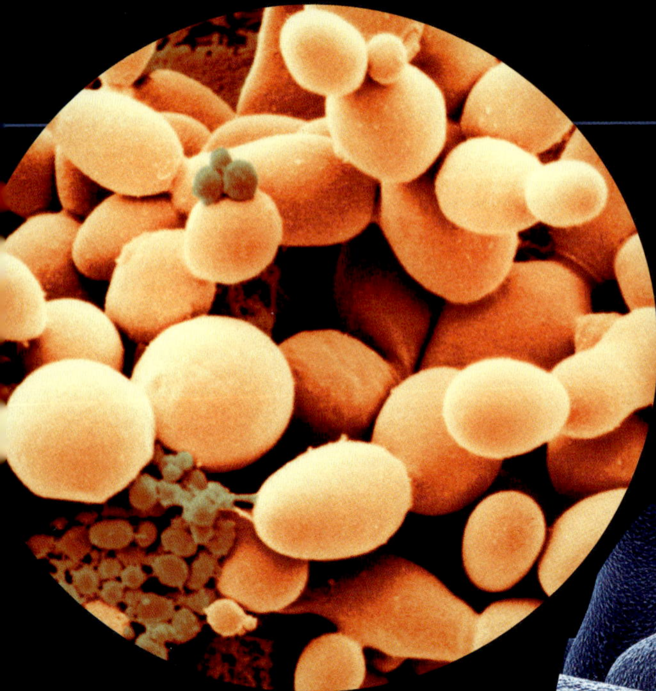

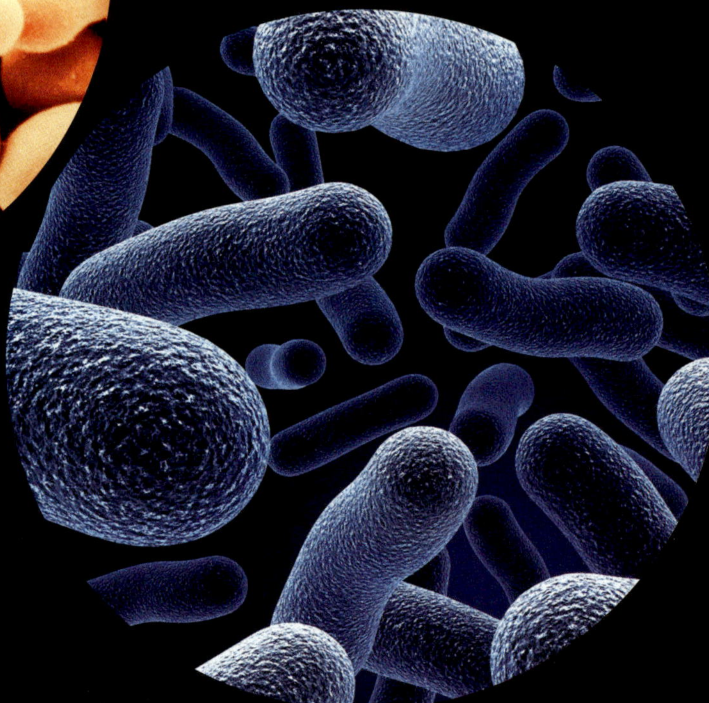

The Work of Microorganisms

Pasteur came up with a new **theory**. He presented it to others. It was a major advance in science. He said that **microorganisms** cause fermentation. Microorganisms are living things. They are too small to be seen with the human eye. Two common types are yeast and bacteria. They can be seen with a microscope. Pasteur also wrote that certain types of microorganisms cause certain kinds of fermentation. Yeast causes alcohol to ferment. A different microorganism would produce something else. That is why some of the living things helped to change sugar to alcohol. Others were ruining it.

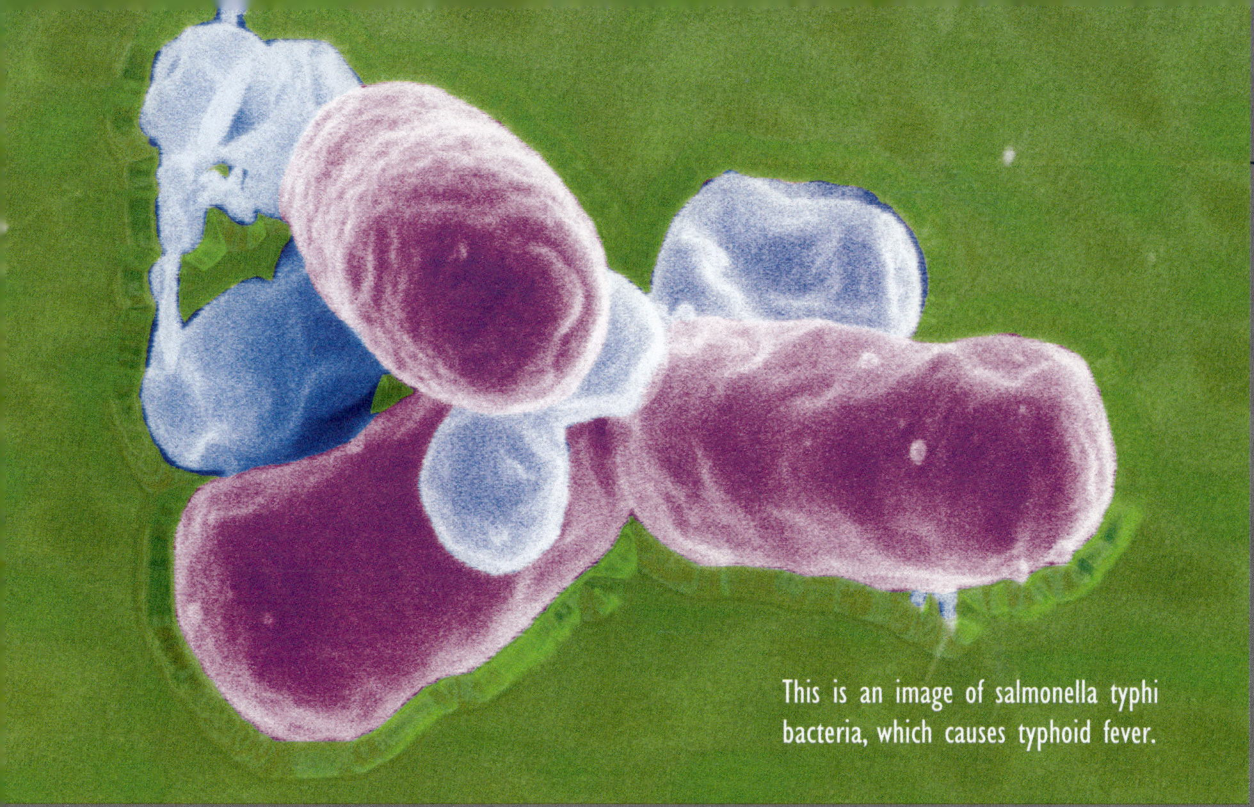
This is an image of salmonella typhi bacteria, which causes typhoid fever.

Typhoid Fever Strikes

By the age of 35, Pasteur was famous around the world. He went to work for the school in France where he had earned his doctorate degree. It was called the École Normale Supérieure in French. He was named director of scientific studies. He continued his research. He was sure that microorganisms caused fermentation.

Pasteur's oldest daughter became sick with typhoid fever. At that time, people did not know how to treat the disease. She died at the age of nine.

Some say his daughter's death made Louis Pasteur want to continue his research even more. He wanted to find a cure for disease.

Today there is a **vaccine** to prevent typhoid fever. We also know that pasteurizing milk can stop germs from spreading. So can drinking clean water. Having clean hands when touching food is important, too.

This boy is getting a vaccination to prevent disease.

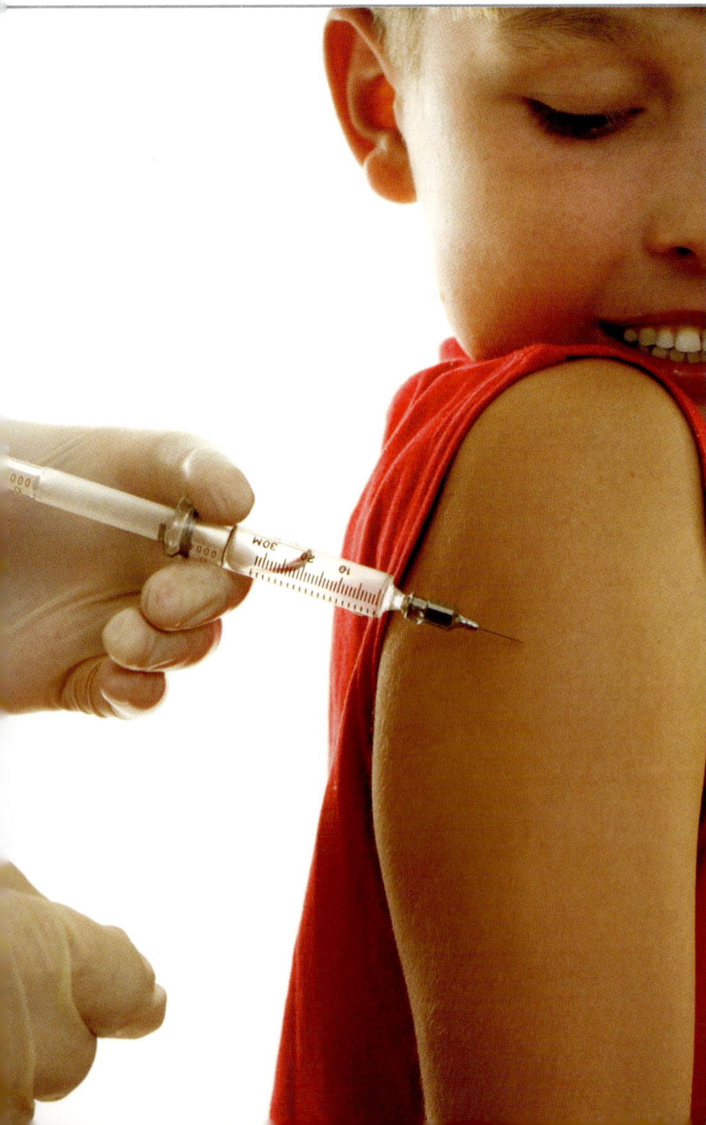

Tough Conditions

When Louis Pasteur took the position at the school, he did not have a lab to work in. He soon found two rooms to use. He turned them into labs. The roofs were low in these rooms. He couldn't stand up straight while working. He had to crawl into the rooms on his hands and knees because they were behind the stairs.

Training Teachers

The school in Paris was named École Normale Supérieure. That means "higher teacher training school." It was an advanced school for teacher training.

Spontaneous Generation

Someone wrote a book about spontaneous generation. This was a scientific theory. It said that living things like mold and germs came into being all the time from things that are not living. The author believed that this theory was correct.

The Academy of Sciences started a contest. It wanted scientists to prove the theory right or wrong. It would pay the scientist who could do the best job. Pasteur entered. He won the contest and the money. He showed that the theory was wrong. He did this by proving that food rots when it comes in contact with germs in the air. When food is kept separate from living germs, it does not change.

These images show rotting bread, grapes, and a close-up of rotting raspberries.

Graceful as a Swan

Have you ever seen a swan-necked flask? These containers played an important role in some of Pasteur's experiments. The glass flasks had necks that were shaped like an *S*. Pasteur would boil the liquid inside the flask. He would then leave them unsealed. Because of the shape, no microorganisms were able to get to the liquid. They were getting trapped in the bend of the *S*. That meant that the microorganisms could not get to the liquid. The liquid stayed pure.

Teacher Knows Best!

Pasteur had a chemistry teacher in school. He had made a suggestion to Pasteur. He told him to use the flasks for his experiments. Good thing he listened to his teacher!

a swan-necked flask

Saving French Industry

Pasteur used his findings to help wine makers in France. Sometimes the wine they made would be fine. Other times it would become sour.

Pasteur found something in the sour wine. He found it had a certain kind of bacteria in it. This bacteria is the same one that helps to create vinegar. It was making the wine go sour.

Pasteur began to heat the wine. This killed the bacteria that were making it sour. All wine was then heated.

The worker near this pasteurizing machine wears protective clothes. The clothes protect the liquid from germs carried on the person.

spinning silk from silkworm cocoons

They called the process pasteurization. Today, many kinds of drinks are pasteurized. This stops them from going bad.

The government asked Pasteur to do something. It wanted him to look into diseases that were affecting silkworms. Silk making was a big business in France. Within three years, he found two diseases causing the problem. He was able to stop the illness from spreading.

Pasteurized Milk

Almost all the milk we buy today is pasteurized. It has been heated to 161.6 °F for 15 seconds. This process kills the harmful bacteria in the milk.

a silkworm moth

The Cause of Disease

Almost 20 years passed after Pasteur's daughter died. Remember, she had died from a disease. Pasteur began to study diseases. He wanted to know what caused them. He had a theory. He thought that microbes caused many diseases. Different microbes caused different diseases.

Microbes could make humans sick. They could also make animals sick. Pasteur studied sick animals. He noticed they would only have an illness once. Once they had an illness, they would not have the same one again.

He used this information to create vaccines. He took the germ that caused the illness. Then he made it weak. Next, he injected it into the animals. This protected them from future illness. Pasteur found a way to vaccinate a herd of sheep. This was to protect them against a deadly disease called **anthrax**. He also saved chickens from a disease called **cholera** (KOL-er-uh).

anthrax bacteria spores

Pasteur innoculated vaccinated sheep with anthrax. The vaccinated sheep did not get anthrax.

Anthrax

Pasteur found that anthrax bacteria make **spores**. They can live for centuries in soil. Anthrax is usually fatal in animals.

Pasteur told people that he had found a vaccine. No one believed him! So he did an experiment in public. He gave 25 sheep the vaccine. He did not give it to 25 others. Then they were all exposed to anthrax. The sheep that had the vaccine lived. The others died. Pasteur's vaccine is the same one used for humans.

Anthrax spores are more deadly than the bacteria. When people inhale them, they get ill fast. They often die. If anthrax spores were used as a weapon, many would die. When a plant in Russia leaked spores, 66 people died.

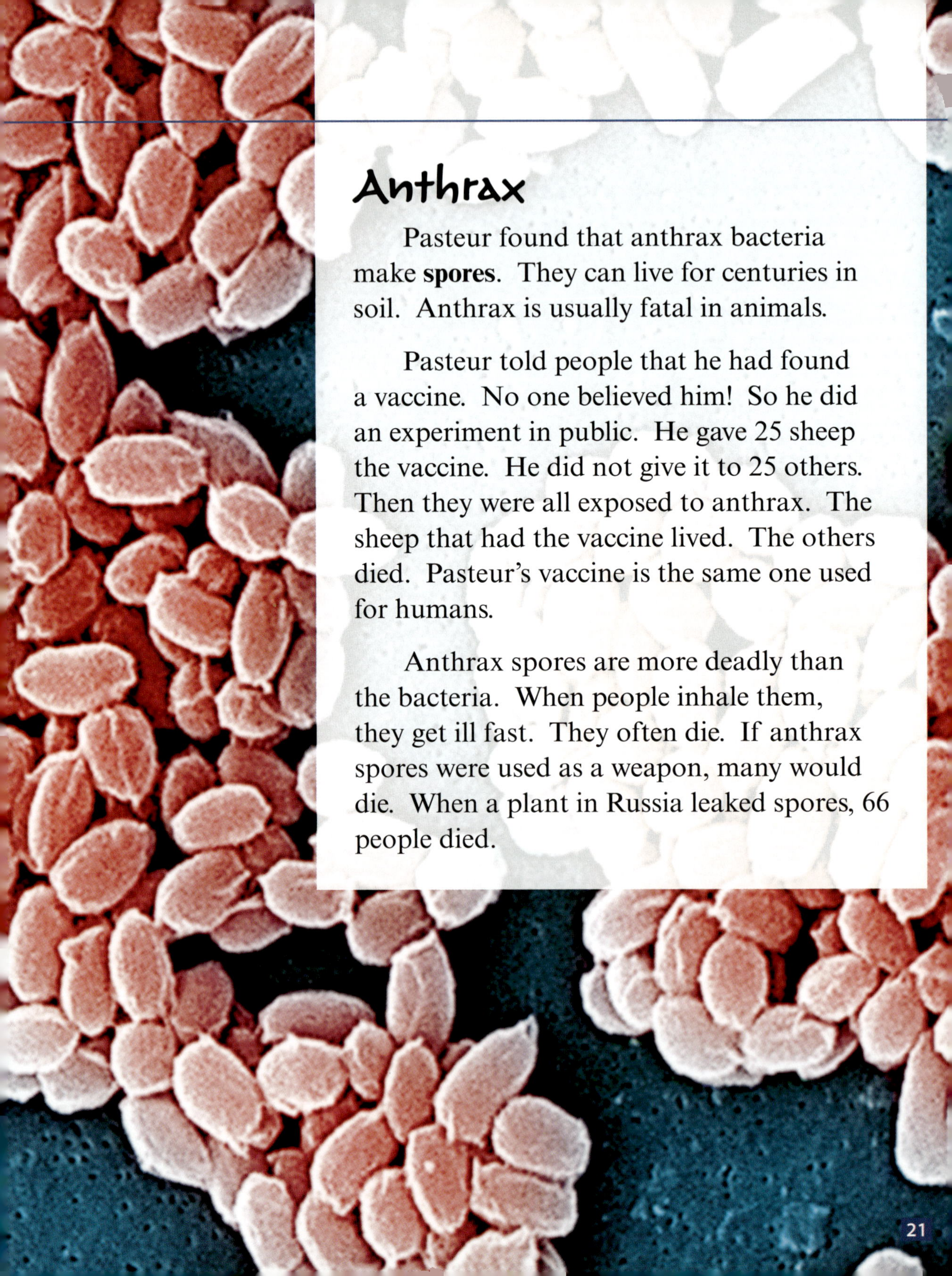

Finding a Cure for Rabies

Pasteur studied **rabies**. Rabies is a deadly disease. People can catch it by being bitten by an infected animal. Pasteur wanted to make a vaccine. He wanted to protect people from this disease.

Pasteur first tested his vaccines on 50 dogs. None of them became sick. He was ready to try his vaccine on people. He gave the vaccine to a boy who was bitten by a dog. The dog had rabies. Without treatment, the boy was sure to die. After he received the vaccine, the boy lived. The vaccine was a success!

Over the next year, more than 2,000 people were given the rabies vaccine. Today, we use the rabies vaccine to protect our animals. We also use it to protect ourselves from the disease.

Pasteur is shown surrounded by English doctors, nurses, and young patients who received the rabies vaccine.

Vaccine Source

Pasteur made his rabies vaccine shots from the dried spinal cords of rabbits.

A doctor gives an unhappy child a vaccination in the 1800s.

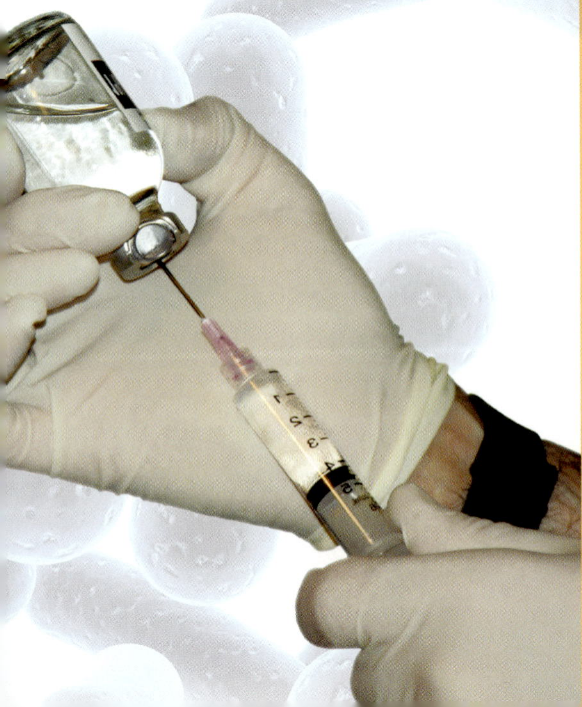

Vaccines

Vaccines have been developed for many things. They protect people from many illnesses. In the United States, most children are given vaccines soon after birth. This keeps them from getting diseases that were once common.

In 1967, people all over the world began getting the vaccine for smallpox. The disease was gone 10 years later. The chicken pox vaccine started being used in 1995. The polio vaccine began being used 40 years earlier.

Louis Pasteur in his later life

The Pasteur Institute

In 1888, the Pasteur Institute was opened in Paris. It was a center for treating and studying rabies. Pasteur acted as its head. He was there until his death. Today, the Pasteur Institute studies many **infectious** diseases. Its scientists have been awarded Nobel Prizes in science.

Pasteur died in 1895. He was 72 years old. His work has helped people around the world. He gave us pasteurization. He showed that microbes cause disease. He developed the rabies vaccine.

Pasteur was a pioneer in the field of microbiology. His work has helped to save countless numbers of lives. He will be remembered for so many things. Above all, he will be remembered as one of the greatest scientists of all time.

Pasteur at the Movies

A movie was made of Louis Pasteur's life. The movie was called *The Story of Louis Pasteur*. It was made in 1936.

An actor plays Pasteur in the 1936 movie.

the Pasteur Institute in Paris

Sally Ride Science

Microbiologist: Rita Colwell

University of Maryland

Microbe Hunter

Rita Colwell is a hunter. But she doesn't hunt animals. Instead, Colwell hunts microbes. Most microbes are harmless, but some can make people sick. They are very tiny living creatures that are too small to be seen without a microscope.

Where does Colwell look for microbes? Everywhere! Microbes can be found in water, air, soil, and other living things, including people. "I learn how microbes live in the environment, and how they can cause disease," Colwell says.

While working in India, Colwell learned that many people were getting sick from drinking water. It had dangerous microbes in it. She discovered how the microbes got into the water. Then she taught people how to pour water through cloth before drinking it. The cloth captured the microbes, making the water safer to drink!

"I like making discoveries that help people stay healthy."

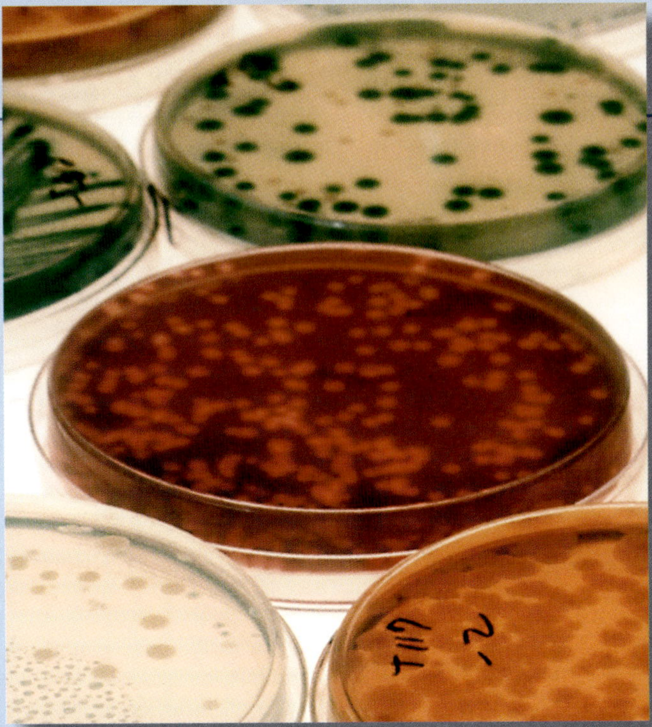

Evidence of microbe activity is in these petri dishes.

This satellite image shows world water temperature.

Being There

If you were a microbiologist, you would study microbes—microscopic organisms—and their effect on other living things. You might also . . .

- learn about viruses and how they invade cells.
- discover new microbes.
- make medicines to cure disease.

How Do They Know?

When Colwell looks for microbes in the ocean, she uses pictures taken from space for clues. One clue is dark spots in the water that could be a large group of microbes. Colwell also checks the ocean's temperature and color. High water temperatures and strange color in a patch of water, like red and orange, may mean that microbes are lurking there.

4 U 2 Do

Colwell figured out a simple way to stop people from getting sick from microbes in drinking water. Colds are caused from microbes, too. What are some ways to prevent your family and friends from catching a cold?

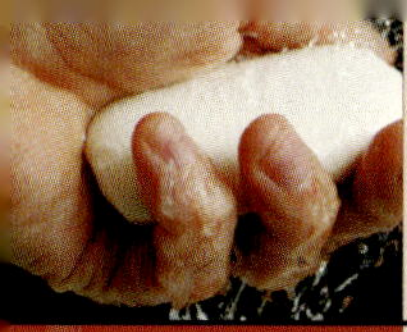

Let's Experiment

Lab: Preventing the Spread

In this experiment, you and your partner will test how effective handwashing is in preventing the spread of germs.

Materials

- chart paper
- marking pens
- apron or smock
- washable paint
- timer or watch
- sink
- blindfold
- towels
- soap

Procedure

1 Create a comparison chart. Divide a sheet of paper into four sections with a marking pen. Draw an outline of a hand in each section. Shade in your idea of a hand that looks completely dirty, very dirty, dirty, and a little dirty. Label each section. Also, create two scoring charts. Label one Water. Label the other Water and Soap.

2 Choose one person to be the hand washer. Choose another to be the timekeeper.

3 Have the hand washer cover his or her hands with washable paint. Let the paint dry completely.

# of Infection

Go to the sink. Put a blindfold on the hand washer. Have the washer run his or her hands under water for one second. Have the time keeper dry the hand washer's hands by lightly touching the towel to the skin. (Do not rub off the paint.) Compare the washer's hands with the chart. On the Water scoring chart, record how clean the washer's hands are.

Have the washer wash for four more seconds with water. Again, lightly blot the washer's hands. Record how clean the hands are.

Have the washer wash for 15 seconds more with water. Blot and record the cleanliness.

Take the blindfold off. Allow the washer to completely clean his or her hands. Put the blindfold back on. Repeat steps 2 through 5, only this time have the washer use soap each time. Use the chart labeled Water and Soap.

Change roles. Repeat the activity until everyone has had a turn being the hand washer. Have the same person keep time.

Display your results. Create two graphs showing the average cleanliness score at each time interval. One graph will show the results when using water only. The other graph will show results when using water and soap.

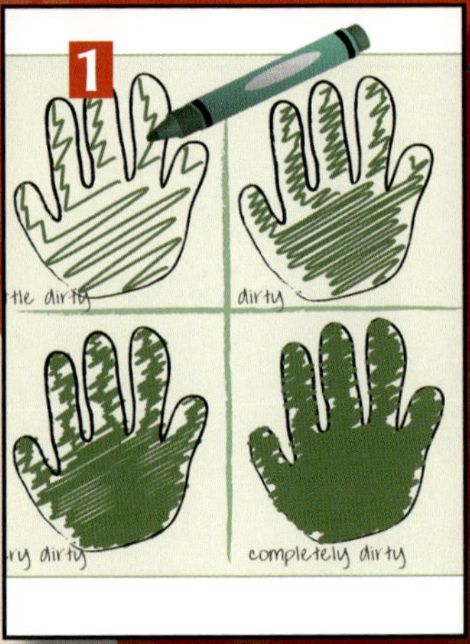

Glossary

anthrax—a kind of bacteria that causes deadly disease

bacteria—single-celled organisms that live in soil, water, organic matter, or the bodies of plants and animals

chemistry—the science of substances and their reactions

cholera—a type of bacteria that causes a deadly disease of the stomach

crystals—solids formed by the solidification of a chemical, and having a highly regular atomic structure

fermentation—changing sugar to carbon dioxide and alcohol through a process involving yeast

infectious—able to cause an infection, or make sick

microbes—a tiny life form, especially bacteria that causes disease

microbiology—the branch of biology that deals with tiny life forms (microorganisms) and their effects on other living things

microorganisms—a life form that is too small to see, especially bacteria

microscope—an instrument used to make very small objects appear larger

mold—plants that make spores instead of seeds to reproduce

pasteurization—heating a drink or other food to kill microorganisms that can cause disease, spoiling, or unwanted fermentation

professor—a college teacher specializing in a certain area or field of study

rabies—a deadly disease that can infect most warm-blooded animals, passed on by the bite of infected animals

spores—single-celled reproductive bodies that grow into new organisms

tanners—people who change animal skin into leather

theory—a set of beliefs used to explain a group of facts

typhoid fever—a deadly disease caused by bacteria and passed on mostly by dirty food or water

vaccines—microbes that have been killed or made weak and given to people to stop them from getting serious illness

yeast—a type of fungus which is used in making alcoholic drinks, such as beer and wine, and for making bread swell and become light

Index

Sally Ride Science

Sally Ride Science™ is an innovative content company dedicated to fueling young people's interests in science. Our publications and programs provide opportunities for students and teachers to explore the captivating world of science—from astrobiology to zoology. We bring science to life and show young people that science is creative, collaborative, fascinating, and fun.

Image Credits

Cover: North Wind Picture Archives/Alamy; p.3 Sebastian Kaulitzki/Shutterstock; p.4 (top) Sebastian Kaulitzki/Shutterstock; p.4 Photos.com; p.5 Pascal Goetgheluck/Photo Researchers, Inc.; p.6 (top) Keith Lamond/Shutterstock; pp.6–7 Leonard Defrance/Getty Images; p.7 (left) Tim Bradley; p.7 (bottom) Mikko Pitkänen/Shutterstock; p.8 (top) Laurence Gough/Shutterstock; p.8 POPPERFOTO/Alamy; pp.8–9 Photos.com; p.10 (top) Olga Shelego/Shutterstock; p.10 Mary Evans Picture Library/Alamy; p.11 (left) ultimathule/Shutterstock; p.11 (right) Todd Gipstein/CORBIS; p.12 North Wind Picture Achives/Alamy; p.13 (left) SciMAT/Photo Researchers, Inc.; p.13 (right) Tischenko Irina/Shutterstock; p.14 Dr. Gary Gaugler/Photo Researchers, Inc.; p.15 Leah-Anne Thompson/Shutterstock; p.16 LockStockBob/Shutterstock; p.16 (left) LockStockBob/Shutterstock; p.16 (right) Leo/Shutterstock; p.17 Charles O'Rear/CORBIS; p.18 (top) Paul Reid/Shutterstock; p.18 Holt Studios International Ltd/Alamy; p.19 (left) Joris van den Heuvel/Shutterstock; p.19 (right) Maria El-Kotob/Shutterstock; p.19 (bottom) Emilia Kun/Shutterstock; p.20 Stefano Bianchetti/CORBIS; p.21 Scott Camazine/Alamy; p.22 POPPERFOTO/Alamy; pp.22–23 (back) Sebastian Kaulitzki/Shutterstock; p.23 (right) Bettmann/CORBIS; p.23 (left) Michael G. Smith/Shutterstock; p.24 Library of Congress; p.25 (top) First National Productions/Getty Images; p.25 (bottom) Maasha/Flickr; p.27 (top) Dan McCoy/Getty Images; p.27 (bottom) NASA; p.28 (top) Mariusz Szachowski/Shutterstock; pp.28–29 Nicolle Rager Fuller

Making It Go

The Life and Work of Robert Fulton

Don Herweck

Physical Science Readers: Making It Go: The Life and Work of Robert Fulton

Publishing Credits

Editorial Director
Dona Herweck Rice

Associate Editor
Joshua BishopRoby

Editor-in-Chief
Sharon Coan, M.S.Ed.

Creative Director
Lee Aucoin

Illustration Manager
Timothy J. Bradley

Publisher
Rachelle Cracchiolo, M.S.Ed.

Science Contributor
Sally Ride Science

Science Consultants
Michael E. Kopecky,
Science Department Chair,
Chino Hills High School
Jane Weir, MPhys

Teacher Created Materials
5301 Oceanus Drive
Huntington Beach, CA 92649-1030
http://www.tcmpub.com

ISBN 978-0-7439-0578-7

Table of Contents

Always an Inventor

Robert Fulton is best known for creating the first successful **steamboat**. That is really just a small part of what he did. He was an inventor, artist, statesman, **mechanic**, and **engineer**. From the beginning, he spent his days learning and trying new things.

Fulton was born in Pennsylvania in 1765. His father died when he was just three. His mother was left to raise him and his siblings alone. When Fulton was just eight, his mother sent him away to school. But she became worried. She didn't think he was learning enough there.

She told his teacher of her concerns. The teacher said there wasn't much he could do. He thought that Fulton's "head was so full of original ideas that there was no room for . . . the contents of dusty books." Fulton didn't want to learn about what others said and did. He wanted to figure things out for himself.

Laws of Motion

Every engineer must learn the **Laws of Motion**. Sir Isaac Newton first came up with them about 300 years ago. They explain the effects of **force** on motion. The first law says that an object at rest will stay at rest if there is no outside force to put it into motion. It also says that a moving object will keep going in a straight line at the same speed forever unless there are outside forces. The second law says that a force makes an object speed up or slow down. The third law says that if a force is used, something happens in response to it that equals its power.

Force is needed to make planes take off, fly, and land.

Fulton began to invent things when he was a young boy. When he was 13 years old, he made his own pencils. He used sheets of lead. Pencils were not new at that time. But Robert's pencils were just as good as the **graphite** pencils that were invented before this time.

Fulton was very smart, but he never did well in school. He learned how to read and write at home. He did not like to do his schoolwork. He wanted to work at the mechanics shop instead.

Gunmaker

Fulton was an expert gunmaker, too. When he was a teen, he made parts for gun makers.

As a boy, Fulton made his own pencils.

Early Engineers

Engineering has been around for a long time. It is the use of science and math to design, build, and operate buildings, machines, and systems. Heron of Alexandria was one of the first engineers. The exact date of his birth is unknown. But some experts believe he was born around A.D. 75. He is worth noting because he made a steam engine that helped a great deal in developing the first jet engine.

In addition to working in mechanics, Robert was an artist. In fact, as a young man, his dream was to become a painter. In 1786, he went to London to study art. Making a living as an artist was difficult. So, he returned to his engineering work. He used his artisitic skills to sketch his inventions.

An important thing to note about Fulton is that he did more than just think of new inventions. He also designed and built most of his ideas.

Fulton was quite the artist. This is one of his sketches, *Cruelty Presiding over the Prison Ship*, done in 1856.

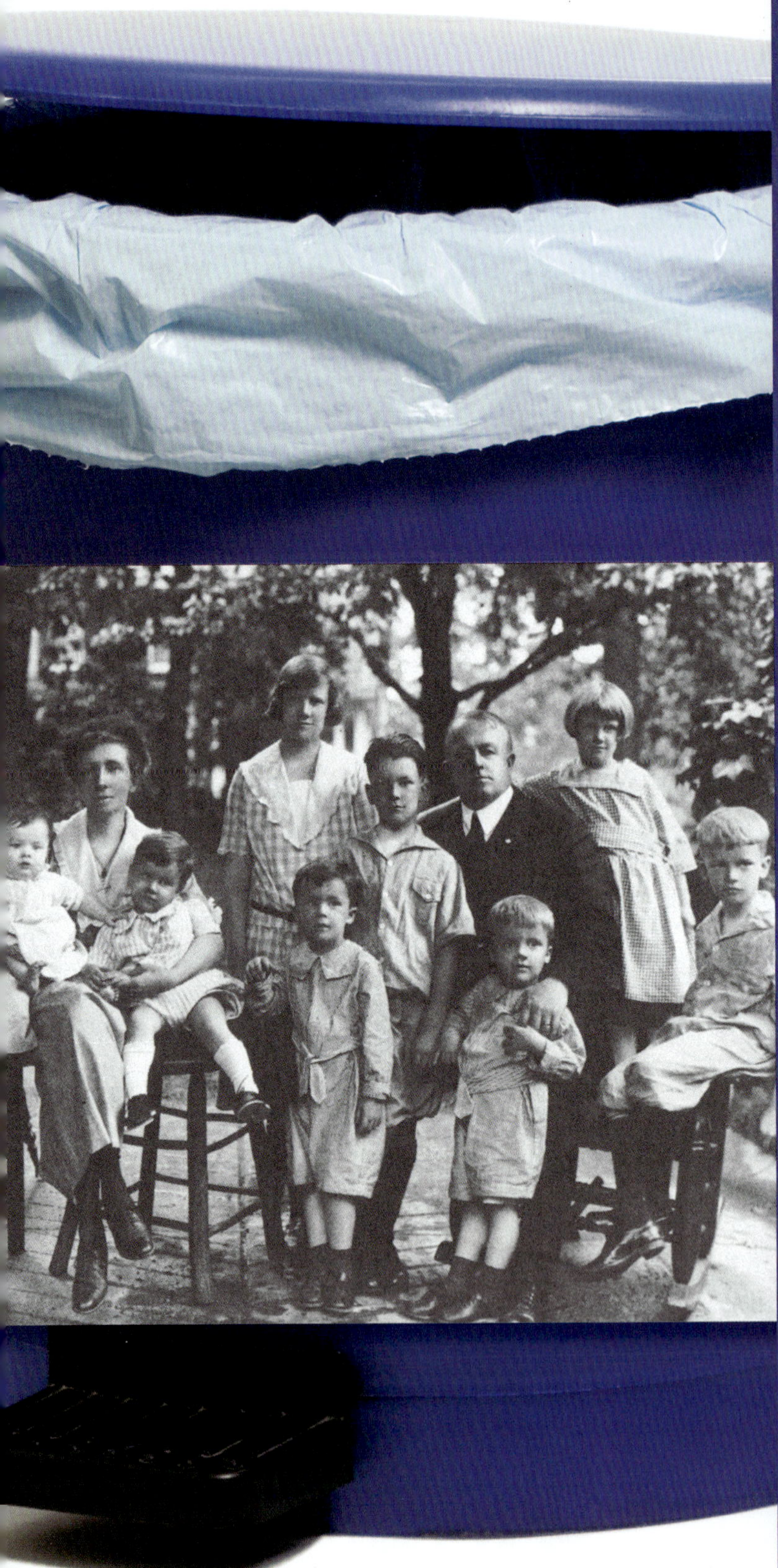

Lillian Gilbreth

Lillian Gilbreth was born in 1878. She earned degrees in literature, but she became famous for other things. First, she had twelve children. One of them wrote the famous novel **Cheaper by the Dozen** about their family. The second is that she became an important engineer. During the Great Depression, Gilbreth helped the president of the United States find ways to make work more efficient. She also invented many things you use every day. These include the foot-pedal trashcan and refrigerator door shelves. Gilbreth was also the first woman elected to the National Academy of Engineering. She lived to be 94 years old.

Working with Boats

Robert Fulton always liked boats. He spent much of his life looking for new ways to propel boats through the water. The fishing boats of his time moved by "poling." This was done by pushing a long pole against the bottom of a river. Robert wanted to make a better boat. He designed a boat with paddle wheels and a crank. The boat did not look very nice, but it worked well.

Here you can see the hand crank used to paddle the boat and the rudder used to steer it by.

Paving the Way

In 1918, Kate Gleason became the first female member of the American Society of Mechanical Engineers.

Martha J. Coston

They say that necessity is the mother of invention. They also say that you can do anything you set your mind to. Martha J. Coston proves that both are true. When she was just 21, her husband died. She was left to care for their four children alone. It was the mid-1800s. Coston didn't have many options. She found plans for a **signal flare** in her husband's notes. She took his idea and made it better. Coston used the **technology** of fireworks to help make bright, safe, long-lasting flares. The U.S. Navy gave her $20,000 for her invention. With that money, she started an engineering company. It lasted until the late 1970s.

Making Them Better

Robert Fulton often worked to improve earlier inventions. Most people think he invented the **steam engine**. The steam engine had actually been invented before Fulton's work. Fulton, however, was the first to put the design ideas into action. He studied the ways that steam could be used to move boats through the water. In 1807, Fulton built the *Clermont*. It was the first steamboat that could be called a success.

Measure Up!

Any good engineer knows that nothing can be done without good measurements. Fulton had to be exact when it came to building his steamboat. These are his measurements for the *Clermont*.

Length: 43 meters (142 feet)
Maximum height: 19 meters (62 feet)
Maximum width: 4.3 meters (14 feet)
Draught: 4.8 meters (15 feet 9 inches)
Displacement: 1,210 tons
Average Speed: 4.7 miles per hour
Distance Traveled: 150 miles in thirty-two hours

Early Steam Engine

Thomas Savery (1650–1716) built the first steam engine. It was used to pump water out of coal mines.

Canals

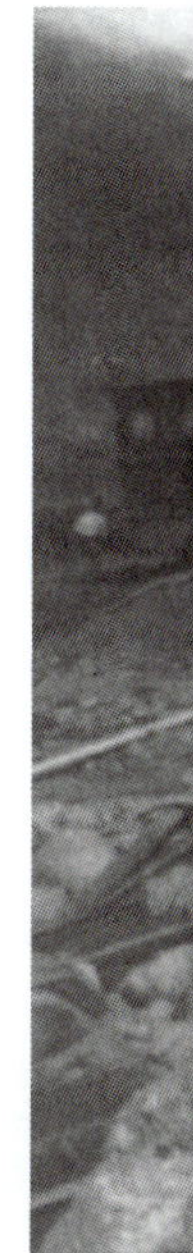

In 1796, Fulton wrote a paper about **canals**. Canals are waterways. Fulton thought small boats on canals would be better than carts and horses on roads for transporting goods and people. So, he designed new types of canal boats. He also thought of a way to drag boats up hills between canals. Water wheels and pulleys were used to do this.

British leaders liked Fulton's ideas. They needed canals to move coal from mines to the city. Fulton was hired to make the canals in England better.

This image shows a modern lock system at work.

Construction of the Panama Canal

Canal to the World

Canals help move heavy loads over water. The Panama Canal allows ships to move between two oceans. A French engineer started to build it in 1878. The United States finished it in 1914. In 1999, the United States gave Panama control of the canal. Today, the Panama Canal is used to shorten the routes of commercial ships. Also, cruise ships use it to move between the Atlantic and Pacific Oceans.

Panama Canal locks in 1913 before it opened to ship traffic in 1914

Robert Fulton continued his canal work for many years. One important invention that improved the use of canals was the double inclined plane. This could be used to raise and lower boats in and out of canals. An **inclined plane** is shaped like a wedge. It allows heavy loads to be raised with less energy. A load would be much harder to lift without it.

Fulton showed how one plane could be used to raise a boat. The other plane was used to lower a boat at the same time. Fulton's design used water as the energy source. It also used pulleys with chains to connect the two boats. This was a very useful invention!

Fulton's double inclined plane made it much easier to lower and lift boats into and out of the water.

Canal Clean Up

In 2005, Hurricane Katrina struck. It caused a lot of damage. Much of the damage was caused because the levee systems failed. Whole neighborhoods were flooded. That's when engineers like Karen Lahare stepped in. She managed a huge canal clearing project in the state of Louisiana. She and her team cleared more than 112 kilometers (70 miles) of canals.

Pyramid Planes

Inclined planes were used to build the pyramids in Egypt. Egyptians used inclined planes that were over a mile long.

Diving Boats

Fulton wondered about underwater travel. How could it be possible? He wanted to find a way. In 1800, he made a diving boat. It was made of wood and metal. Water put into tanks would add weight to it. This weight would push the boat down. When water was pushed out of the tanks, the boat floated up.

Fulton built a dome on top of the boat. The dome had thick windows to see through. The crew would get in the boat through the dome. A hand crank turned a propeller. This powered the diving boat underwater.

Does this kind of vehicle sound familiar? Fulton's diving boat is what we now call a **submarine**.

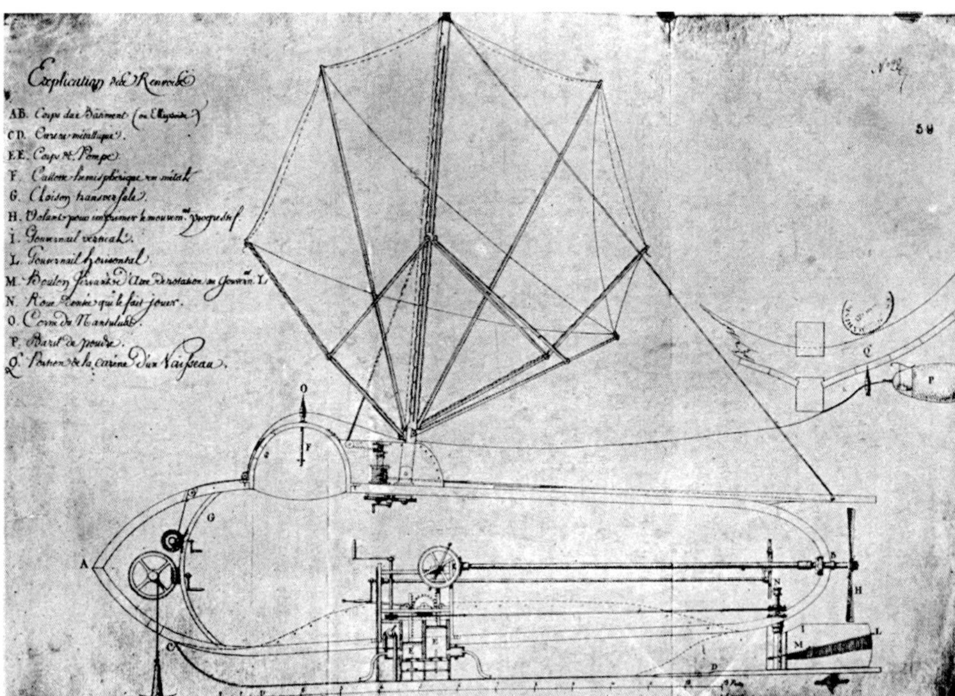

Fulton's diving boat

Modern submarines

Submarines

Submarines have changed a lot over time. In 1954, the first nuclear-powered submarine was made. It can stay under the water for a long time. Sailors can live for months below the sea in such a submarine. Modern submarines have changed **warfare**, too. Early submarines had to come to the surface to fire missiles. Submarines today can fire missiles under the water. Submarine missiles can travel long distances to their targets.

It was Napoleon, the great leader of France, who asked Fulton to design the first practical submarine. The model he built was called the *Nautilus*.

Fulton gave his diving boat design to French leaders in 1801. He planned the **hull** to be armored. That would protect it from cannonballs. The boat was designed to have a small crew of sailors. They would turn a crank to move the boat. The crew had to raise a mast and sail when above water. Fulton used a **compass** to direct the boat under the water.

Fulton led tests with a group of three men from the government to review his plans. Fulton and the others remained under water for three hours. They were able to raise and lower the boat by filling and emptying water from tanks. The boat could go to depths of nearly 8 meters (25 feet). The pressure of the water any deeper would have crushed the hull.

Naomi Leonard

Dr. Naomi Leonard is a modern engineer. She recently received a big award to continue her work: $500,000. The money is known as a "genius grant." It was given to her because she shows so much creative and original thinking in her work. She designs ways to control robot vehicles under the water. These vehicles are sent to patrol the seas. They can stay for long periods of time—much longer than a human can. While there, they gather data about sea life. The data they get can help to reveal what happens deep beneath the surface.

Maritime Warfare

Robert Fulton lived during a time of many wars. At that time, the British navy ruled the seas. Fulton wished for world peace. Yet, he combined many of his inventions to make weapons. Fulton hoped his weapons would end wars. He tried to sell his weapons to both the United States and countries in Europe. He thought in this way he could help to bring peace.

Fulton put underwater cannons onto boats. Before that time, cannonballs were shot onto decks of other ships. They put holes in the ships or damaged the sails. The ship would sink or slow down. Fulton's new cannons could shoot into the sides of ships. This would put holes in the ships under the water level. Water would then rush into the ships' hulls. This made the ships sink faster.

Fulton also made torpedoes with gunpowder that could explode underwater. He designed his diving boat to tow the torpedoes. His boat could tow a torpedo under a ship and then set the fuse. This would blow up the ship's hull and sink the ship.

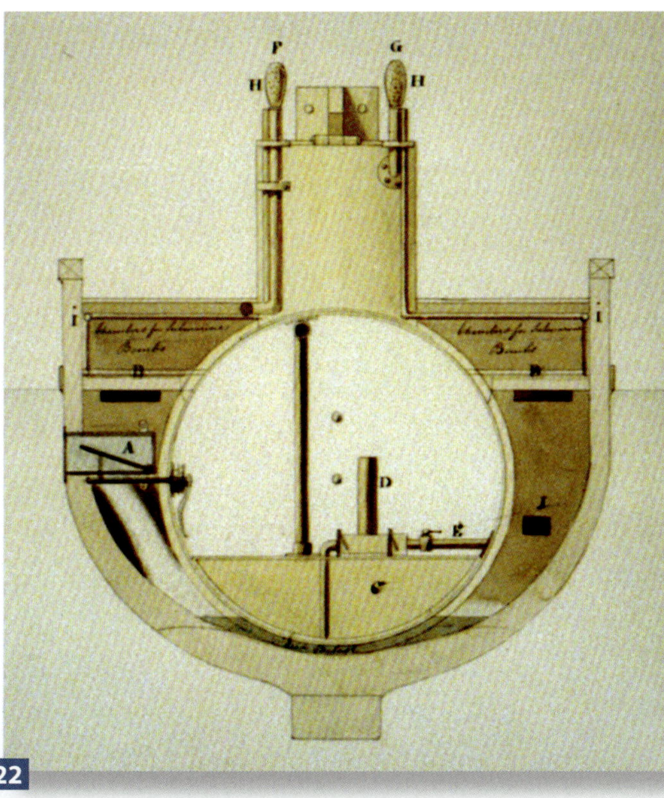

This sketch done by Fulton in 1806 shows a cross section through a "plunging boat."

Engineering the Brooklyn Bridge

John Roebling was hired in 1867 as the chief engineer of the new Brooklyn Bridge project. An accident at the site led to his death in 1868. His son Washington took over. When he became ill in 1872, his wife Emily took on the job. She supervised the day-to-day construction. Many of the workers thought of her as the chief engineer. She had already studied some of what she needed to know before the project. She also learned much on the job. She became such an expert that many bridge workers sought her advice. She worked on the bridge until it opened in 1883.

Later Life

Little is known about the personal life of Robert Fulton. Many books have been written about him. Each of these mainly gives a long history of his inventions. A few things are known.

In the later years of his life, Fulton was put in charge of all steamboat traffic in New York. Steamboats were commonly used to transport people. He charged high fees because he had all the steamboats. In 1818, other people began to run steamboat businesses. Now there was competition. This dropped the price of fares. Fulton's company could not stay in business.

At one time, steamboats did the work that modern ferries do today.

Some of New York's waterways today

Fulton did not live a long life. He developed lung problems that started with a bad cold. He became very sick. In 1815, at the age of 49, he died in New York. It is said that his death "deprived the United States of one of her most useful citizens."

Robert Fulton spent his life as an inventor, mechanic, and engineer. His work lives on in his inventions. It also lives in the work of engineers that came after him. Even today, engineers use his work to develop ideas and inventions of their own.

Roboticist: Cynthia Breazeal

Massachusetts Institute of Technology

Bot Buddies

Meet the woman who could make *Star Wars* real. "I saw *Star Wars* when I was really young," Cynthia Breazeal says. "I really adored R2-D2 and C-3PO. Having robots like that someday captivated my imagination."

Becoming an astronaut and going to Mars also captured her imagination. Breazeal started designing robots that might one day explore Mars.

Now she designs robots like the furry guy below named Leonardo. He's programmed to behave like a friend.

When Breazeal is not in the lab, you can find her surfing or snowboarding. "When I was growing up, I was probably known much more as an athlete than as a scholar." Maybe someday she'll design a bot to join her on the slopes.

Robots like Breazeal designs can be used for both work and play.

Is It 4 U?

If you were a roboticist, you might . . .

- design machines that build cars.
- build hi-tech toys.
- program robots to explore Mars.

4 U 2 Do

Do you think you'll ever play sports against a robot? Draw a picture of what a robotic athlete might look like.

Lab: Pressure, That Sinking Feeling!

Mechanical engineers must know all about the way things work in order to design, build, and run them. For example, a submarine engineer must figure out how to make a boat submerge or float. Without this information, the submarine will be useless.

Try this lab to learn something about floating and submerging. You will be on your way to becoming a mechanical engineer!

Materials

- a clear plastic bottle with a tight lid, such as a water bottle
- a squeeze condiment packet, such as for ketchup
- a glass
- water

Procedure

1. Fill a glass with water.
2. Place your unopened condiment pack into the water. The packet should just barely float. If it sinks, try another type of packet.
3. After you have a good packet, fill a clear plastic bottle with water.

4 Put your unopened condiment packet into the bottle.

5 Screw the top on the bottle.

6 The condiment packet is now a "boat." Squeeze the bottle to make your boat submerge, or go downward.

7 To make your boat rise, simply relax your hand.

What Is Happening?

The bottle filled with water has pressure in it. The condiment packet has a small pocket of air in it. When the bottle is squeezed, the air pocket in the condiment packet is made smaller. This is similar to adding water to the ballast tank of the diving boat or submarine. The increased pressure pushes the boat downward. The decrease in pressure brings it back up.

Glossary

canal—a long channel of water artificially made for boats to travel along

compass—a device for finding direction using a freely moving needle that always points to magnetic north

engineer—to plan, build, or manage a building or construction project

graphite—a soft shiny black carbon that is used in making lead pencils

hull—the body or frame of a ship, most of which goes under the water

inclined plane—a simple machine for elevating objects

Laws of Motion—Sir Isaac Newton's three basic laws that describe the affects of force on motion

mechanic—someone whose job is repairing the engines of vehicles and other machines

signal flare—a very bright light or colored smoke which can be used as a signal, or a device which produces this

steamboat—a boat which moves by steam power

steam engine—an engine that converts the heat energy of pressurized steam into mechanical energy

submarine—a ship which can travel under water

technology—the application of science, especially to industrial or commercial objectives

warfare—military fighting between enemies

Index

Sally Ride Science

Sally Ride Science™ is an innovative content company dedicated to fueling young people's interests in science. Our publications and programs provide opportunities for students and teachers to explore the captivating world of science—from astrobiology to zoology. We bring science to life and show young people that science is creative, collaborative, fascinating, and fun.

Image Credits

Cover Getty Images; p.3 Photos.com; p.4 (top) Library of Congress; p.4 (bottom) The Granger Collection, New York; p.5 Photos.com; p.6-7 The Granger Collection, New York; p.7 (left) Johanna Goodyear/Shutterstock; p.7 (right) Costin Cojocaru/Shutterstock; p.8 (top) Public Domain; p.8 (bottom) The Granger Collection, New York; p.9 (back) Diego Cervo/Shutterstock; p.9 (front) The Granger Collection, New York; p.10 (top) Photos.com; p.10 (right) Tim Bradley; p.10 (left) Scott Laumann; p.11 (top) Scott Laumann; p.11 (bottom) Leo/Shutterstock; p. 12 (top) Tim Bradley; p.12 (bottom) Library of Congress; p.13 (left) Tim Bradley; p.13 (right) Mary Evans Picture Library/Alamy; p.14 (top) Israel Pabon/Shutterstockp; p.14 (bottom) Photos.com; p.15 (top) Library of Congress; p.15 (bottom) Library of Congress; p.16 (top) The Granger Collection, New York; p.16 (bottom) Library of Congress; p.17 (bottom) The Granger Collection, New York; p.18 (top) Library of Congress; p.18 (bottom) The Granger Collection, New York; p.19 (top) Harald Høiland Tjøstheim/Shutterstock; p.19 (left) Danilo ducak/Shutterstock; p.19 (right) Library of Congress; p.20 (top) Photos.com; p20 (bottom) Bettmann/Corbis; P. 21 (front) courtesy of Naomi Leonard; p.21 (back) Alexis Rosenfeld/Photo Researchers, Inc.; p.22 (top) Library of Congress; p.22 (bottom) Library of Congress; p.23 Photos.com; p.24 (top) Carsten Medom Madsen/Shutterstock; p.24 (bottom) Library of Congress; p.24–25 Photos.com; p.26 Sam Ogden/Photo Researchers, Inc.; p.27 Jason Grow; p28 Danilo ducak/Shutterstock; p.28–29 Nicoll Rager Fuller; p.32 Getty Images